Enacting Community Economies Within a Welfare State

Published by Mayfly Books. Available in paperback and free online at www.mayflybooks.org in 2020.

© Teppo Eskelinen, Tuuli Hirvilammi & Juhana Venäläinen (eds.) 2020

Layout by Mihkali Pennanen (based on earlier MayFly book layouts by Kaajal Modi).

Cover photo by Maia C from Rebecca Louise Law's *Community* exhibition (Toledo Museum of Art). Photo's license: Attribution-NonCommercial-NoDerivs 2.0 Generic (CC BY-NC-ND 2.0)

ISBN 978-1-906948-51-1 (Print)
ISBN 978-1-906948-52-8 (PDF)
ISBN 978-1-906948-53-5 (ebook)

This work is licensed under the Creative Commons Attribution-Non commercial-No Derivatives 4.0 International (CC BY-NC-ND 4.0). To view a copy of this license, visit http://creativecommons.org/licenses/by-nc-nd/4.0

Enacting Community Economies Within a Welfare State

Teppo Eskelinen,
Tuuli Hirvilammi &
Juhana Venäläinen (eds.)

Contents

Authors vi

Acknowledgements xi

1. Introduction: Community economies and social transformation with, within and beyond the welfare state........... 1
Teppo Eskelinen, Tuuli Hirvilammi & Juhana Venäläinen

2. The conception of value in community economies............... 23
Teppo Eskelinen

3. Diverse work practices and the role of welfare institutions..... 47
Tuuli Hirvilammi & Maria Joutsenvirta

4. Building upon, extending beyond: Small-scale food production within a Nordic welfare state 71
Pieta Hyvärinen

5. Commoning surplus food in Finland – actors and tensions ... 95
Anna-Maria Isola and Janne Laiho

6. Self-organised online ridesharing as a 'transport commons' .. 117
Juhana Venäläinen

7. Epilogue: On the possibilities to learn from the Global South............ 143
Laura Kumpuniemi & Sanna Ryynänen

Bibliography... 152

Authors

Teppo Eskelinen is a senior lecturer at the Department of social sciences and philosophy, University of Jyväskylä. Having obtained his PhD in philosophy (2009), he moved to teach social and public policy and subsequently development studies. His multidisciplinary research covers a variety of themes, chiefly related to the normative and political aspects of the economy: global justice and extreme poverty, economy/ics as power, alternatives to growth/capitalism, and heterodox economics. He has also published on themes such as development policy, radical democracy and the possibility of utopias. In general, Eskelinen hopes his academic work to retain the transformative spirit of the global justice/solidarity movements which originally drew him into having an interest in societal matters.

Tuuli Hirvilammi is a postdoctoral researcher who currently works at the Faculty of Social Sciences at Tampere University, Finland. Her academic background is in social policy but her long term aim has been to integrate sustainability concerns into social policy as well as into wellbeing research. She believes that multidisciplinary research and learning from alternatives is a key answer to radically transform our current societies. Her research interests include sustainable wellbeing, eco-welfare state, ecosocial policies, degrowth and ecological economics which is seen in her publications she has co-authored both for the Finnish and international readers. Besides the academic research she is a degrowth and timebank activist, even though lately she has been more occupied as a local politician in her hometown.

Juhana Venäläinen is an assistant professor in cultural studies at the University of Eastern Finland, Joensuu. His research revolves around fractures and new formations of work and the economy. In and after his doctoral thesis (2015), he has strived to explore how the notion of "the commons" could recalibrate understanding of the value-creating processes in contemporary capitalism, with case studies ranging from silence tourism to the affective economies of googling. Venäläinen has edited volumes and special issues e.g. about employment precarity, the experience economy and financial cultures. Lately, he has focused on the paradoxes of "sharing" and "gig" economy.

Pieta Hyvärinen is a doctoral researcher in gender studies at Tampere University, with an academic background also in environmental politics. Their research concentrate on small-scale food production from the perspective of feminist postcapitalist economics and interspecies relations. In their doctoral thesis in the making, they develop a concept of multispecies livelihoods to elaborate the interdependencies and contradictories in everyday food production practices. So far they have authored journal articles on communal agriculture and urban beekeeping, co-authored book chapters on translating and teaching diverse and community economies, as well as co-edited a special issue on naturecultures in feminist studies. Along with research and writing, small-scale food production also plays a minor role in their everyday life as a hands-on practice.

Anna-Maria Isola is a Research Manager at The Finnish Institute for Health and Welfare. Her research has covered the politics of breastfeeding, experiences of poverty and experienced inclusion, and population-political rhetorics – on which topic she obtained her PhD in 2013. She leads a research group that has developed and validated the Experienced Social Inclusion Scale (ESIS) -indicator. Anna-Maria's thinking is that the welfare state continuously needs to renew itself; however the renewal can only happen sustainably when economic systems change as well. Change processes are global, but solutions are first found locally. "Think globally, act locally" describes her thinking well.

Maria Joutsenvirta is a Senior Research Fellow affiliated with the Sustainability-in-Business (SUB) program at Aalto University School of Business (https://people.aalto.fi/maria.joutsenvirta). She is interested in finding answers to how economy can be harnessed to serve ecological and social wellbeing through, for example, practice of commons, new 'monies' and systemic co-design. She has used post-growth and heterodox economics lenses to detach wellbeing and societal structures from the extractive, growth-dependent economy. Maria believes that a sustainable future demands a shift in the way people and organizations relate to one another and with the Earth. Her academic and practical work aims to foster deeper and more meaningful relationships between people, with nature and with our own inner worlds.

Laura Kumpuniemi is a doctoral researcher at the University of Eastern Finland. At the moment, she is working on her PhD thesis about political and democratising aspects of solidarity economy in Bolivia. In her research she is interested in exploring the possibilities of post-capitalist politics, post-development practices, and local and global networks of reciprocal solidarity. In Finland, she is active in an organic food cooperative and in the network and communication group called commons.fi. Laura is also passionate about fostering global networks of solidarity in practice and in her activism she has worked especially with Latin American countries and Western Sahara.

Janne Laiho is a film-maker and marketeer. He is especially interested in the application of art (particularly film) for communicating societal change and issues. With degrees in economics (MBA) and art (M.A.), he has been able to examine market economy dynamics through art. The Family Federation of Finland, The Finnish Youth Research Society, and The Finnish Institute of Occupational Health have commissioned Janne to produce documentary films on societal topics. These films have been parts of larger, academic research initiatives; the role of these films in the research initiatives has been both to uncover new information as well as to communicate dynamics that are hard to communicate by other means.

Sanna Ryynänen is a senior lecturer at the Department of Social Sciences, University of Eastern Finland. Her academic background is in sociology, and her PhD she obtained in educational sciences, specialising in social pedagogy (2011). Her research topics range from social inequalities, processes of marginalisation and excluding bordering practices to belonging and citizen participation, as well as to social and political theatre as an invitation to political discussion and dialogue. In her research, she often experiments with creative and participatory research methods, and believes in the transformative potential of academic work and research. Her interest in solidarity economy comes with her long history in Brazil, and her research in this field focuses on the pedagogical dimensions of solidarity economy and solidarity economy incubators as pedagogical and political actors.

Acknowledgements

As becomes hopefully evident to the reader, this book is not so much a collection of individually authored articles, but first and foremost an outcome of a collective effort. This effort was not a brief one but involved a seemingly endless sequence of meetings filled with ideas, discussion and collective inspiration. Therefore, it is necessary to mention a missing author of this book: Tuomo Alhojärvi was part of the collective all along. The fact that he eventually withdrew from article writing does not diminish his claim to authorship of this book.

The institutional background of this book was a Kone Foundation-funded project investigating rights, exclusion and social production of value in alternative economies. This not only provided time to focus on research for some of the authors but also a platform in the sense of venues for meeting and planning. Indeed, sometimes the best possible support for research is a possibility to withdraw to a guesthouse in a nature reserve area with one's colleagues.

MayflyBooks took a positive approach to our project from the very beginning and has provided us with highly valuable feedback. We appreciate the co-operation with the publisher. Warm thanks also to Marcus Petz, who did the language revision for the book. We were lucky to have a proofreader who has an excellent command on the subject matter in addition to his native language skills.

1
Introduction: Community economies and social transformation with, within and beyond the welfare state

Teppo Eskelinen, Tuuli Hirvilammi & Juhana Venäläinen

This book is an exploration of community economies within Nordic welfare states. Even though the upsurge of community economies is typically discussed in the context of countries plagued with economic problems, we currently see active movements building community economies in the wealthy and stable countries of the Nordic region as well. As a countermove to the increasing penetration of capitalist market relations into all spheres of life, including spheres in which public service provision used to be dominant, people in Nordic welfare states are building co-operatives that foster small-scale production, new value-based networks such as timebanks, and various kinds of local arrangements for creating and sharing resources collectively.

Amidst the threatening ecological crisis, people are seriously looking for economies that will be more sustainable, and ultimately, support a socially more meaningful life. What we indeed need is a different value conception and more localised economy, instead of mere 'redistribution'. Instead of accepting the destructive patterns and hierarchies penetrating the economy as we know it, we are looking for economic forms that are based on horizontal relations and the principle of equity. As concrete alternatives to capitalist forms of production, community economy initiatives represent to many minds a qualitatively better way of seeing and enacting the economy. We see these emerging community economies not as marginal curiosities but as great sources of inspiration on what 'the economy' fundamentally could signify, both in theory and in practice (e.g. Healy 2009).

The agenda for scrutinising the tension between community economies and Nordic welfare states is two-fold. First of all, we need a systemic and case-driven analysis of how community economies emerge on the outskirts of the welfare state model, a model which is in flux. Community economies often emerge by harnessing and repurposing the potent 'surplus' that the public service provision generates, and serendipitously filling the gaps that inadequate provision leaves unserved. Second, we need to see, how community economies directly challenge the ways in which welfare states currently develop, proposing new trajectories of societal change and alternative ways of framing this change. Both aspects relate to the relationship between community economies and welfare state institutions, and inform questions such as: On what terms can community economies and Nordic welfare states co-exist and cooperate? Could a Nordic welfare state be an enabling platform for community economies to diffuse? And, crucially: Could community economies show the welfare state its desirable future model?

Introduction

Community economies and diverse economic relations

But what exactly do we mean by 'community economies'? Following J. K. Gibson-Graham, community economies refer to the ongoing democratic co-creation of the diverse ways in which we collectively make our livings, receive our livings from others, and provide for others in turn (e.g. Gibson-Graham and Community Economies Collective 2017). In Gibson-Graham's vocabulary and within the social movements inspired by them, a community economy does not refer simply to a 'local business activity', but to an 'ongoing negotiation with all life forms'. The approach highlights the process in which socio-economic relations are continuously coproduced (Community Economies 2019). Community economies exist for things (production, organisation) to be done differently. They exist for the sake of self-organisation, non-hierarchical relations and direct interaction. Thus community economies aim to 'make real the possibility that the economy can be a space of ethical action, not a place of submission to "the bottom line" of the "imperatives of capital" as it is so often portrayed' (Gibson-Graham and Roelvink 2011, 29). So, while community-based economic forms have existed throughout history, we use the term 'community economies' with a more intentional, even political tone. We see community economies exactly as politics in a concrete form.

In addition to monetised market relations, economic relations include alternative market relations and non-market relations, alternative paid labour and unpaid labour. They include exchanges based on socially transformative values. The already existing 'spaces-beyond-capitalism' are diverse and relational (S. Wright 2010, 299). According to Ethan Miller (2013), community economies are constructed by three interconnected moments: the ontological, ethical, and political. Within the ontological moment, both the content of 'the economy' and 'the community' are in still in flux: the economic 'figures as an 'open-ended discursive construct' organising a vast, heterogeneous field of relations' (Miller 2013,

521). The ethical moment opens a space for negotiating ethics: the questions of livelihood and interdependence' (Gibson-Graham 2006b, x; cited in Miller 2013, 523). Lastly, in the moment of politics, the 'positivity [i.e., a positive, normative understanding of the community's objective] is collectively enacted' (Miller 2013, 525). Our case studies move between the ethical and the political moments: they serve not only the purpose of illustrating the heterogeneity of economic practices in general, but they also open spaces for ethical discussions and develop into collective political projects.

Community economies come in many forms, some primarily institutionalising a new form of currency, others a new form of exchange, yet others a new kind of community. Some might mostly attempt to decommodify a given sphere of life. Examples discussed in this book range from food production and distribution (Chapters 3–5) to harnessing vacant car seats through online mediated ridesharing (Chapter 6), and further to the managing of cultural and community spaces and services (Chapters 2–3). What is common to this wide set of projects and initiatives is that they not only setup institutions, but are also performative examples of economic versatility, manifesting the general notion of diversity of economic systems. Furthermore, while all systems have some articulated purposes, reasons to engage in community economies are versatile. For some people, reasons for participation are very practical: access to otherwise inaccessible goods and services, forming social contacts, and for others even survival. Springing from these motivations arise a diversity of economic relations which we aim to endorse with the concept of community economies. Indeed, the notion of 'diverse economies' is used throughout the book to refer to this general plurality or forms, purposes and motivations.

In any case, the ontological and social basis on which community economies operate can be seen as distinct. Usually, it is referred to as 'the commons' (e.g. De Angelis 2017). Commons systems comprise not only of collectively managed resources, but also of social subjects or actors that manage them (commoners) and the cultural practices of commoning that sustain the productive cooperation. While the concept of commons is far from restricted to community economies, community economies can be seen exactly as instances of establishing a commons as a sustainable and equitable system, the organisation of which deviates from the logic of the modern state. The notion of commons is helpful for analysing tensions such as inclusion/exclusion and complementariness/co-optation in the process where community economies take functions that have been understood as core welfare state competencies. Commons systems are based on a radical conception of inclusiveness that surpasses the citizenship-based universalism of the welfare state. As Stavros Stavrides (2016, 38–39) argues, commoning only retains its defining dynamics if 'always expanding beyond the limits of any community that gives it ground and develops it', a feature that presupposes 'an ever-expanding community of potential collaborators'.

However, this principle of spontaneous and open-ended collaboration can be a double-edged sword when portrayed as an alternative to public services, rather than as a complement to them. For example, when commons-based peer production steps into the arena of safeguarding minimum subsistence (Chapter 5) or providing minimum transport services throughout the country (Chapter 6), there is a risk of community economies being used as what De Angelis (2013) calls a 'commons fix': an arrangement where the existence of grassroots-level mutual aid becomes a justification for the deterioration of the universal provision of public services.

Approaching community economies in the context of Nordic welfare states

So far, the discussions on the diversity of economic systems and on community economies have mostly focused on organising community economies (e.g. Wright 2010; Seyfang and Smith 2002). The research on diverse economies has less often connected the analysis of the local economic practices to the study of the state and the broader cultural and social structures through which diverse economies are performed (Jonas 2013). However, economic alternatives do not and cannot exist in a social vacuum but interact with their surroundings. To better understand the transformative role of community economies, the task is to see the existing and potential place of such systems beyond their 'niches', or 'protective spaces' (Smith and Raven 2012), in constant interaction and friction with governance outside them.

Community economies function across a wide range of social systems. Why, then, to focus on their relationship with the Nordic welfare state? This is due to various reasons. First, the welfare state is not just a system of governance but also a kind of 'real utopia', clearly being an inspiration especially for the Anglo-American left. Its long history has always included the promise that through state-organised regulation of capitalism, given social rights will be realised and welfare can be guaranteed universally. At least on the level of policy ideas and normative goals, the Nordic welfare states have sought to maximise human well-being within capitalism, or to enable 'socialism within capitalism' (Kloo 2015; Iqbal and Todi 2015).

A feature that has made Nordic welfare states special and different from conservative or liberal welfare regimes (Esping-Andersen 1990) is the strong emphasis on universalism: indeed, the very legitimacy of the welfare state is connected with the universal provision of high-quality services. Furthermore, universal public services and a comprehensive social security system have decommodified everyday lives: when the state guarantees a minimum income and social protection, a person becomes less dependent on capitalist relations. Public services such as libraries, education systems or universal health care that are produced by municipalities and financed on tax revenues, can be seen as 'spaces-

Introduction

beyond-capitalism'; spaces where all have an equal access regardless of the ability to pay. The welfare state has helped to create various kinds of social commons – or, at least, proto-commons: platforms upon which collective grassroots socio-economic cooperation is possible.

Second, the focus on the current welfare states provides an interesting case to explore the ongoing 'penetration of capitalist market relations' to new spheres of life and new policy fields. Despite the inspirational ideas, the contemporary realpolitik of the welfare states sees the idea of decommodification fading away. If the welfare states were always largely capitalocentric in terms of being based on capitalist value creation, its current form is ever more often a state pervasively intertwined with capitalist accumulation and productivist labour markets. Numerous elements of Nordic welfare states have become qualitatively different from the golden era of welfare state expansion in the 1980's, or early 1990's in the Nordic countries.

The hegemony has put emphasis on the 'post-industrial pressures' to welfare states, including globalisation, decline of manufacturing production, the health and pension costs of ageing populations, and changing household and family structures (e.g. the steady rise of single-person and lone-parent households in all Nordic countries). Marketisation, through which market mechanisms such as competition, economic incentives and private provision, are implemented in the public sector, is increasingly offered as a solution to improve quality and economic efficiency of the welfare states (e.g. Moberg 2017). In addition to concrete actions prioritising private market actors, the marketisation trend has taken more subtle forms in the public discourse when the focus is put on social investments, economic incentives and economic productivity of public services. Consequently, the welfare institutions are geared towards competitiveness and narrow-minded cost containment. As this causes institutional uniformity and lack of political manoeuvring space, one can critically ask if this context allows any room for economic diversity?

It is hardly an exaggeration to say that the current Nordic welfare states have largely given up on the goal of decommodification. While of course continuously producing services, this production takes increasingly often a market form in its production and organisation (e.g. Moberg 2017). Such services can be useful and necessary, but they do not contest the market imperative. So much of the attempts to recreate community economies can be seen as efforts to create decommodified spheres, in a situation when the state is losing its interest in providing such spheres. As the chapters in this book reveal, the current capitalist welfare states may not always give a warm welcome to the efforts of community economies to provide decommodified spaces.

Furthermore, the current Nordic welfare system emphasises 'individual responsibility', which means that cash benefits are less generous, more conditional, and more adjusted towards targeting and means-testing. Nordic welfare states have adopted 'activation' policies with entitlements restrictions and activation programmes with sanctions. This has led to the recommodification process in which the income of citizens has become more dependent on the fluctuations of the labour market than it was during the decommodifying expansion phase of the welfare states. (See McCashin 2016; Farrants and Bambra 2018.) Yet these changes have not taken place as abrupt, 'shock doctrine' style social engineering, but rather gradually, as a subtle 'recalibration' of welfare institutions. Despite this transformation, the welfare state ideology appears to be rather resilient: amidst all the cuts to social protection, retrenchment policies have remained unpopular.

The outcome of all this is an interesting conflict between the ideal or the ethos of the welfare state, and current policies within the welfare states. This distinction and tension between the ethos and the institutionalised form of the welfare state serves as a one starting point for our analysis: what is the role of community economies in reviving the ethos and pushing it further? Looking from the other side, the literature on community economies has been quite silent on potential similarities with the welfare model on the level of ideas. This nexus clearly calls for scrutiny.

Ecological limits
The focus on community economies in the Nordic welfare states is highly relevant amidst the fundamental transition that is required for creating ecologically sustainable welfare models. The most pressing challenge of all Nordic welfare states is the current situation where high social outcomes have been achieved at the cost of grave overproduction that exceeds biophysical boundaries. For example, carbon emissions, material use and land use per capita overstep the sustainable limits. (Neill et al. 2018.) Mitigating climate change requires urgent action. Overcoming this challenge calls for reconsidering the relationship between welfare states and capitalist economies. Is economic growth an inalienable part of the welfare state? Has the titubant ecological balance proven that the promise of the welfare state is over? The answer appears to depend on how the relation between economic growth and the fundaments of the welfare state is seen.

Nordic welfare states were developed hand-in-hand with capitalist economies. The golden era of welfare state expansion was also an era of high GDP growth. Therefore, it is possible to argue that welfare systems are instrumental for the growth paradigm and useful catalysts for capitalist reproduction. Even social transfers can be seen to ultimately support the economic growth model and thereby also the ever-increasing consumption possibilities. And in turn, Nordic welfare states depend on economic growth because of the intertwined patterns of productivity, employment, taxation and social spending (Kloo 2015). In this reality, any economic downturn generates social ills.

However, this is not the only possible interpretation. Even if the welfare state as we know it undeniably depends on growth and contributes to increasing (over)production, this dependency might be undoable. We call for rethinking the growth-dependency of welfare states and draw on degrowth research that has shown how the economy could steadily decline in a controlled fashion without catastrophic outcomes on unemployment and poverty (Victor 2012). This might require the implementation of new welfare institutions like taxation on resources and energy, work time reduction, universal basic income, maximum income and public control over the creation of money (Kallis et al. 2012; D'Alisa et al. 2015). It is possible even to argue that the postgrowth reality with the need for new welfare institutions is already here: the high-income welfare states are devoid of new engines of growth, having to learn to live with a stagnant or contracting economy – and make the best out of it in terms of quality of life.

The questions regarding the possibility of a welfare state not based on continuous economic growth remains a debated subject (see e.g. Bailey 2015; Buch-Hansen 2018). Some welfare institutions might indeed be more able to adapt to non-growth conditions, and certainly many welfare functions would remain in a degrowth scenario. Yet this speculation is not our point here. The bottom line is that to comply with the challenges created by the ecological crises, two fundamental changes are in any case needed. First, there will have to be more locally organised, fossil-free economic forms, more commons-based economies, and more small-scale economic systems; second, the welfare state will have to assume forms which foster decommodification. Consequently, the question emerges, how can the relative share of non-growth-dependent activities expand. Community economies thereby fit the picture by creating sustainable economies as well as spaces, platforms and livelihoods that render a life despite growth socially meaningful and materially more possible.

As the welfare state goes through changes, new questions emerge concerning not only scarcity but also abundance. The old welfare states have become abundant with material goods, and as an outcome of this, they produce various kinds of leftovers and excess. An interesting issue is then, how should this excess be seen? Is the production of excess a sign of success or failure of the welfare state? Two chapters in this book take excess as their specific starting point, with two very different kinds of examples: leftover food (Chapter 5) and vacant car seats (Chapter 6). Harnessing excess for the purposes of community economies might lay the ground for new forms of social interaction.

On the other hand, it might as well be a sign that the universalist ethos of the welfare state is crumbling. In the emerging commons systems or commons-like systems, there is always interaction and metabolism between the commons, state and market systems. The new commons are not entirely self-reliant, but are in many ways dependent on the intentional or arbitrary benevolence of the welfare state: the different forms of state-provided subsistence that can be used for building meaningful community economy activities. At the same time, the newly created community economies – such as the network of ridesharing groups – are always prone to be captured and used as prototypes by the market actors that directly capitalise on social cooperation (such as the commercial platform economy services).

Local vs centralised

To add yet another element to the analysis, despite its ethos of decommodification, the Nordic welfare state is based on strong state governance, and thereby tends to favour hierarchical, top-down approaches. Yet this does not mean that all kinds of local initiatives could not and would not exist within it. The elaboration of the practices and prospects of community economies within the Nordic welfare states can cast some light on the questions of state power and legal governance in relation to small-scale community economies that are often 'willfully cultivated and fiercely defended' (Wright 2010, 298).

During the expansion phase of the Nordic welfare states, power has been transferred from local associations and governments to central government. Nowadays, centralised power and comprehensive state regulation seem to be partly in contradiction with horizontal community economies when the state imposes top-down rules and regulates communities that are trying to increase their autonomy and self-sufficiency. If community economies function on the grassroot level, the state can be understood at a regime level that is mostly geared towards the status quo. In this case, the state-led governance structure and close interdependency between state actors and capitalist market actors express noteworthy difficulties in accommodating community economies in present Nordic countries. The context being this, state actors will assumedly fiercely protect a status quo instead of a transformative process, especially in a situation where the Nordic states are financially and materially so linked with the capitalist economy. In this case, the centralised power can easily end up in the hands of big corporations instead of local communities.

To be clear, the welfare state is not a definite or fixed system but can take various forms. Generally, we understand 'state' not as a monolithic and static entity but as a concept that refers to multi-layered governance with constant political struggles over parliamentary power and decision making. The welfare state is distinct from the welfare society. As Robson (1976, 7) has written, there are two sides of the coin in a welfare state: 'The welfare state is what Parliament has decreed and the Government does. The welfare society is what people do, feel and think about matters which bear on the general welfare.' Even if this rough categorisation fails to acknowledge the variety of institutions, we find it useful to see state actors as different from 'society'; in our case the active people cultivating community economies. The cases described in this book show a clear gap between 'the state' and 'the society' and a high mistrust of public authorities in general. It is therefore worth asking, what is the proper role of the state- and what spheres of communities should stay outside of state regulation? Is there a risk of 'state penetration' of community economies?

Accommodating the goals of community economies within the state apparatus requires a deep process of democratisation at all levels. This is why the community economies have to be the starting point, as a non-hierarchical logic already exists in their operation. How can this non-hierarchical organisational logic and idea of value diffuse to ever new social relations? Could Nordic welfare states be transformative and open to the values of alternative economies?

Possible approaches of welfare state institutions
While we take the perspective of community economy activism rather than governance as the starting point, sketching possible ways how the welfare state can relate to community economies assists in constructing a general framework for the articles. The ways in which governments in general and welfare institutions in particular can relate to community economies, can be categorised as inaction, creating enabling background conditions, and finally, direct assistance and institutional learning.

Inaction
As community economies often face considerable pressures from the side of government (be it municipal or national), it would be highly tempting to think that government inaction is the preferred response to the ascent of these alternatives. Indeed, actions by government often appear outright interventionist from the perspective of the community economies, so the logical reaction for them is to resort to protective spaces with clear boundaries and distinct operational logics. This is highly understandable in situations in which government intervention threatens the very existence of a community economy. The threat can come for example in the form of a taxation measure disabling the practical functioning, or seizing the space operating as the base for the community economy (e.g. Joutsenvirta 2016).

Yet the operations of community economies do not thrive on the basis of government inaction only. In addition, ostensible inaction can also involve subtle forms of control. Promoting alternative economies can also be used for keeping the unemployed busy or even 'self-employed', when the universalist service provision base has eroded, and an ethos of self-responsibility is enforced. As will be shown in Chapter 3, work practices are more complex than the dichotomic model (activity/inactivity) imposed by governmental social policy allows. There are also ongoing attempts by governments to control community economies through the 'voluntary sector', strategically governed through planning, monitoring, target-setting, financial incentives and other attempts to align the sector with government policies (Eskelinen 2018). This is typical in austerity policies, which are often combined with the active promotion of community development and decentralised governance (Smith 2010; Coote 2011). Especially the selective use of recognition and funding can be used to effectively govern an ostensibly autonomous sphere, particularly when funding comes with strings attached.

Creating background conditions
For the reasons mentioned above, the role of government should perhaps be seen through the perspective of creating (or failing to create) background conditions for community economies to operate. The way in which a government can take a positively enabling role is related, first of all, to the general structure and cultural mood within a society. Often such background factors go without explicit recognition. Because of their very general nature, the interpretation of the mere existence of these conditions can legitimately be seen as inaction; yet these conditions are highly significant for the autonomy of economic alternatives.

This relates particularly to the general societal mood prevalent in fairly equal societies. Several studies have pointed out the strong tendency of welfare state regimes to foster general trust within society (Larsen 2007; Rothstein 2001). This general trust is clearly a factor that contributes to the creation of alternative economic systems, even to their very autonomy. In an atmosphere of high generalised trust, alternative economic systems can be to a larger degree governed with a collectively designed ethical code and internal conflict resolution procedures, rather than having to rely on formal sanctions. For community economies, high general trust represents an element of independence from the government.

It is also easy to point out a number of policies relevant to the autonomy of alternative economies. Collectivisation of social risks is an important policy measure since it would allow public actors rather than market actors to decide on individual wellbeing (Johnston et al. 2011). To mention another obvious example, policies allowing more autonomy for the unemployed are clearly more enabling than strict labour market conditionalities (see also Chapter 3). Alternative economic projects not only attract unemployed people to provide material and social improvements to their condition, but the very existence of an alternative to capitalist labour contributes to the social space of alternatives. Therefore, proposals such as the universal basic income are also proposals for greater autonomy for alternative economy projects (see e.g. Henderson 2017; Wright 2011 on basic income and autonomy).

Some public services might be directly or indirectly useful for the creation of alternative economies, even though this clearly represents a side-effect rather than the purpose of these services. An important example of this phenomenon is the possibility of digital organising. Organisation on digital platforms greatly contributes to the autonomous space of the practices of alternative economies, as this creates considerable ease in organising and fosters community-building. Yet digital platforms only function in conditions of sufficient and pervasive digital literacy, and high internet access rate. Digital literacy is an outcome of long-term education and public policy, while universal internet access provision (as enabled in Finland) represents an explicit and simple choice to provide a high-speed internet access to all with a nationwide broadband and to make computers available for example in public libraries. While technically unrelated, these policies significantly contribute to the conditions of constructing alternative economies.

Direct assistance and institutional learning
Last, and most importantly, a government could seek to assist community economies and learn from them. The concept of 'the partner state' is sometimes used to describe the ideal of the government which actively supports alternative economies. Partner state is not so much an actual form of government, but rather a cluster of policies and ideas whose mission is to empower and protect direct social-value creation (Bauwens and Kostakis 2014). This is of course more of a vision than an observation, but nothing would prevent governments from making an explicit choice to support alternative economic systems with their existing means. Perhaps this could be seen as one aspect of a rearticulation of the welfare state ethos.

Naturally the extent and form of such support can vary considerably, and the boundary between creating background conditions and direct assistance might be fluid. A typical form of support would be the provision of spaces for free or for a symbolic price, as very often community economy organisations need some kind of spaces for functioning. Space belongs to the kinds of things that are relatively easy for the government, particularly municipal authorities, to provide. This of course holds only on the precondition that such authorities can give up the idea that all spaces should generate monetary profit in accordance with market pricing.

Direct assistance also means that the government provides alternative economy actors avenues for participation with real policy significance. This is vital, as sometimes it is easier for governments to take a paternalistic 'do-gooder' approach than actually listen to and learn from alternative politics. The vocabulary that best describes the community economy logic of operation and valuation can be quite foreign to the mindset of governments. Therefore, positive interaction with public authorities requires processes in which the point of view of the practitioners gets 'translated' into public policy. The challenge is that this ought to happen without the hegemonic discourse to co-opt the alternative and radical vocabulary.

A partner state can then be understood as having two functions. First, it is a government which allows experimenting and maintaining 'protective spaces' (Smith and Raven 2012). The partner state as an enabler means maintaining spaces for self-organisation rather than incentivising civic activity towards determined ends such as full-time employment. The partner state should be open to transform itself in order to create social space for the community economies as autonomous entities. Secondly, a partner state should also be understood as a government open to learn from the values of community economies and be willing to reconsider its institutions to adjust to their logic, rather than merely allowing them to operate.

All this being said, a critical note should be added: direct support cannot be automatically taken as positive. Sometimes a good-willing government can also be a government operating too close to the community economy. On occasion, supportive government activity can also be government activity which will become institutionalised thereby creating a norm that is restrictive and in rigidity lacks the adaptive flexibility. Benefiting from a government requires not only goodwill from the side of the government, but also an element of autonomy and distance to the government for the community economy.

One challenge concerning both the state and the hegemonic capitalist economy is their narrow understanding of 'value'. The value model of community economies is discussed in Chapter 2, with a focus on timebanks. No system of governance could of course choose to shift overnight to an economy informed by another conception of value. However, nothing would prevent public actors from asking themselves, what steps they could take toward the direction of such an alternative value model. Fundamentally, if community economies do embody a qualitatively better conception of 'the economic', then wider economic systems should be informed by this conception.

Synopsis of the book
To recap the point so far, we look for strongly sustainable, democratic and horizontal ideas and practices, incarnated in community economies. Furthermore, we are interested in how these initiatives can flourish within welfare states, and also impact their future forms. Therefore we promote the slogan 'with, within and beyond the welfare state', and maintain an insistence on the sharp division between the welfare state and welfare ethos, the latter remaining an inspiration for constructing democratic and sustainable societies. Our mission is not to promote the welfare state as it is but rather to save and rearticulate the ethos that facilitated the original construction of the welfare state and articulated it as a utopia. Or, to put a long story short: our aim is to analyse the tension between given community-based utopias and a presupposed state-based utopia. Community economies are a challenge to the welfare state, which we urge it to address.

This serves as the starting point for the remaining six chapters in the book. All approach the tensions discussed above from somewhat different perspectives. The cases discussed and approaches taken very purposefully reflect the versatility of community economies. Yet geographically, the cases are located within Finland. This is not because interesting cases would not exist within other countries with a traditional welfare state identity, but because they were easy to approach, and because the cases in Finland serve as good examples that can be generalised quite like any others.

In Chapter 2, Teppo Eskelinen explores the notion of 'social value'. While traditionally economic value has been anchored in either labour or market demand, community economies are unique in insisting on a distinct idea of value. This idea is based on interaction, recognition and community; yet it is 'economic' in the sense of facilitating exchange and being embedded in value-storing practices. After trying to state systematically this conception of value, the article moves on to ask, how can a government relate to this conception of value? Can it recognise this kind of value? Can it foster it? Could it, eventually, see itself producing value as understood within current economic alternatives, rather than being stuck with the capitalist conception?

Chapter 3 sees Tuuli Hirvilammi and Maria Joutsenvirta scrutinising the tension between work as understood within diverse economies, and the currently hegemonic ideas and norms of labour and employment. How can people devote their agency and time to constructing alternatives when they also need to survive in a capitalist economy, perhaps being pushed to employment by disciplining authorities? The question is approached by studying individuals who are actively involved in developing alternatives. The chapter takes up two case studies – an art centre and a food cooperative –, through which a repertoire of work practices are analysed. The article asks, what are the practical ramifications of decisions by state actors and welfare institutions on the work practices existing within these alternatives? The findings show how employment policies and social security systems have both enabling and disabling impacts on the possibilities to enact community economies. The chapter then proceeds to discuss, how could the enabling features be strengthened.

Pieta Hyvärinen contributes with an exploration of small-scale food production in Chapter 4. Small-scale food production is a living practice rather than a historical remnant. Furthermore, it should be seen as one of the potential remedies for the threatening ecological crisis, in contrast to the productivist welfare state, which obscures the material basis of food production and sees the expansion of production as the most viable solution to existing problems. Hyvärinen examines small-scale food production in relation to various tensions which unfold from this setting: how can the welfare state be enabling and disabling; what kinds of relations with other species are in operation in the production practices; how does the capitalocentric worldview manifest itself here and how could diversity be promoted?

In Chapter 5, Anna-Maria Isola and Janne Laiho examine food waste as a specific kind of commons. While leftovers can theoretically be freely claimed by anyone, food waste is both a system of living on the surplus of the welfare state, and a contested terrain because of new 'participatory' systems. Currently, there are new initiatives to organise the unemployed to cook together from leftover food. This system combines control of the unemployed, participatory citizenship, and circular resource-efficient economy – in other words both positive and negative aspects. Through an analysis of such systems, the article analyses the colliding and mutually enforcing aspects of the welfare state and the 'leftover commons'. Is the leftover cooking system a way of the welfare state to enforce traditional productivist control over the workforce, or a way to establish a sphere of commons and support increasing independency from the monetary economy?

In Chapter 6, Juhana Venäläinen analyses the self-organised mobility networks created through online ridesharing groups. These systems challenge the traditional public transport services as well as more commercially oriented platforms of sharing. They can then be seen an institutionalisation of ad hoc 'transport commons', such as hitch-hiking. Yet it is an open question, whether such transport commons can really be an alternative to public/commercial modes of transport, rather than being merely complementary. To what extent do they ultimately depend on the existing transport systems? Could institutionalised transport systems be formed on the basis of self-organised transport commons? The article discusses these issues by analysing the hybrid and dichotomous qualities of ridesharing systems, which currently enjoy the freedom to design their rules and practices relatively autonomously.

The concluding chapter is a commentary serving as a postface, written by Sanna Ryynänen and Laura Kumpuniemi. The chapter delves into the issue of whether the northern community economies care to learn sufficiently from the rich traditions of alternative economies of the Global South. Drawing from the experiences in Latin America, Ryynänen and Kumpuniemi point out that economic alternatives might look quite different when they are created for purposes of survival; and the reality of government partnering with community economies might create other kinds of outcomes than we would like to hope for.

Together, the chapters aim at entering a kind of implicit dialogue with each other, or at least providing a collection of viewpoints. The relation between community economies and welfare states is not settled, and one can ask, whether it ever will fully be. But different perspectives can shed light on different scenarios, points of friction, hopes and fears.

2

The conception of value in community economies

Teppo Eskelinen

Conceptions of value state the purpose of economic practices and ultimately steer economic activity, as any social system has a tendency to generate what is seen as having value. Further, a dominant value conception is both *performative* and *ontological*. Performativity means that the associated ideas not only describe, but also shape social reality. Any given dominant conception of value changes social reality so that more of the valuable will be produced. Further, descriptions of value become treated as really existing aspects of social reality and further the only possible descriptions of value – thus 'ontologisation'. Alternatives then appear to counter 'what exists'.

Yet such conceptions are not necessarily conscious but can be implicit. Therefore, an explication of hegemonic value conceptions is needed in order to support alternatives. As stated in the introduction, it is necessary for the purposes of social justice and ecological survival to create more localised, egalitarian and sustainable economic forms. Community economies not only entail non-capitalist *practices*, but also a unique *idea* of what is valuable, and thereby worth doing. Community economies insist on seeing value in social interaction, community, self-organisation and empowerment. This chapter sets out to describe the dominant capitalist value conception, a community economy alternative, and analyse how the welfare state ethos could move in the direction of the latter.

As discussed in the previous chapter, the welfare state is a fluid concept, which can refer either to an ideal (ethos) or really-existing systems of governance. The existing systems do have patterns deviating from capitalism, yet they are becoming ever more penetrated by the markets. From the viewpoint of the theory of value the main question is, whether the self-perception of the welfare state is to *redistribute* value while accepting the capitalist value conception, or to push a value conception which deviates from the capitalist one. As noted, especially the idea of decommodification has been lately on the losing side. Therefore, at best the community economy conception of value can function as a challenge to the welfare state: it could resume the notion of decommodification, and further assume such community economy virtues as limits to growth and the value of social interaction and care. Indeed, the fluidity of the concept of the welfare state should not be understood as an ambiguity, but as an open arena of political struggle. The welfare state can then assume a narrow capitalist conception of economic value and see itself as redistributing this value, or it can see its very essence as based on a broad value conception.

Yet having noted the variance of welfare states, the same needs to be said about community economies. Indeed, the category refers to a range of initiatives and institutions characterised by mere family resemblance. It is consequently difficult to point out *the* definite value conception of community economies. Therefore, I will focus here on one concrete example: timebanks. Timebanks are community-based economies in which *time* is used to calculate the value of a provided service. This is a way of emphasising equality, as no-one's time has more value than anyone else's. Practically, the

2 – The conception of value in community economies

system is based on a centralised system of accounting in which time to provide the services is credited to or debited from the accounts of the provider or recipient, causing the accounting system as a whole to balance at zero. Practically, any timebank member can announce skills or needs on an (often digital) noticeboard and agree on an exchange (either between the parties themselves or mediated by a 'broker'). In addition to insisting on equality, the system sees enhancing community-building as its mission.[1]

Of course, relying on a single case might seem like a limitation and indeed makes general reference to community economies somewhat tenuous. Yet timebanks can be seen as an archetype of a community economy. Furthermore, while they might not exhibit all aspects of the category, they are very explicit about the advocated conception of value. Further, they aim at transformation both in the realm of market exchange and in the realm of social relations, community and participation. The explicit and the transformative aspects facilitate the analysis of their distinctive value conception.

The hegemonic value conception

The capitalist conception of economic value has gained a hegemonic position. Because the hegemonic conception is rarely articulated and more typically just embedded in practices as a given, a criticism and search for alternatives should begin by making the value conception explicit. While this could be done by analysing the daily functioning of the capitalist society, there is also an explicit value conception available: the one articulated in economics. Contemporary mainstream economics is intimately connected with capitalism. Furthermore, it carries major epistemic power because this economics is the science for both describing and reproducing the capitalist order: it is then a system for reflecting, what capitalism sees as valuable.

---

[1] For general introductions to timebanks, see Cahn 2004; Seyfang 2004; Gregory 2015.

The idea of value as it exists in contemporary economics is based on two theories seen as mutually exclusive: the *labour theory of value* and the *subjective theory of value*. More precisely, economics can be seen as being grounded on the demand-based theory of value, so that the justification narrative sees the labour theory of value as the only existing (and conceivable) alternative to it. In other words, the conception of value in contemporary economies is based on these two ideas: first the dominance of the demand-based theory, and second the belief that the theory of value needs to be chosen from these two mutually exclusive alternatives.

Classical political economy, including Ricardo as well as Marx, leaned on the labour theory of value (Theocarakis 2010). The classical economists assumed a theoretical entry point, according to which value refers to the amount of labour embodied in a commodity, including historical labour needed to develop the necessary physical capital. Ricardo formulated the theory as follows: 'The value of a commodity, or the quantity of any other commodity for which it will exchange, depends on the relative quantity of labour which is necessary for its production, and not on the greater or less compensation which is paid for that labour' (Ricardo 1817). 'Labour' is thus a very general term for categorising human productive activity appearing in several societal and historical contexts (Mandel 1990). Furthermore, it is seen as a commensurable substance, which allows the comparability of completely different kinds of goods.

The labour theory of value has been criticised for being ambiguous about the relation between value and price (generally on the subject, see González 2013), or even as metaphysical (Robinson 1962). Yet the most influential criticism focuses on the tendency of labour theory of value to ignore the subjective valuations of market agents, in other words demand. This criticism gave rise to the marginalist school of thought and the subjective theory of value that forms the basis of neoclassical economics. According to this theory, the economic value of a given good is determined by

2 – The conception of value in community economies

the interplay between subjective valuations of goods (expressed though market demand) and the scarcity of these goods. Thus, the value of a given good cannot be objective and constant, like the labour theory of value suggests, but depends on the will of consumers to pay for the good.

The subjective theory of value tends to reduce all theorising on value into market transactions, in which the expressed valuations of atomistic market subjects are decisive. The theory ignores the value of things external to market goods as well as non-commodified goods, as it assumes that valuation has to be expressed within the market, if (economic) value is to exist. Indeed, the social aspect of the economy or value that the theory recognises is the existence of instrumental market relations: people might engage in exchange and contracts as they observe temporary mutual gain. Furthermore, value is seen to be consumed in the instance of transaction: whatever happens to the object after the transaction is a personal issue and beyond the scope of value theory.

On a quick look, the existing value conception, or more precisely the paradigm describing these as mutually exclusive alternatives, might sound sensible. Therefore, a critical look needs to be taken on the particular weaknesses within this conception.

Both labour and subjective theory of value state, that value can be detached from the social basis which enables its production. This has a dual implication: firstly, no social patterns of care, upbringing or such, are recognised as valuable; and secondly, the social process in which economic goods are exchanged, is seen as meaningless from the perspective of determination of value. Moreover, no notion of power is incorporated in the value conception, therefore casting the hierarchies in economic processes or their unmaking as insignificant.

Additionally, the subjective theory of value functions effectively as a justification for capitalist practices, particularly because of what it omits. Two issues in this regard stand out. First off, the subjective theory of value leans on an idea of well-being, according to which well-being is always enhanced when more market preferences are met, thus forming the basis of seeing the limitless growth of consumption as a well-being endeavor means to improve well-being. Secondly, it sets no limits to how much the perceived value of different inputs can be seen to deviate, thereby giving an excuse to any magnitude of disparities.

All this leads to a need to see beyond these apparently exclusive choices. It is not necessary to base the theory of value on either a mechanical reference to the labour time used to produce the good, nor a narrow theory functioning as an excuse for capitalist practices. A better alternative is to ground economic value on the whole process, including reproduction, social interaction as a basis for well-being, together with a notion of limits to growth and consumption. I will now turn to the community economy conception of value as articulated within timebanks, to see how these theoretical points figure in that context.

Characteristics of the community economy conception of value

Mainstream economics appears locked with the ostensible necessity to choose between the labour theory of value and the subjective theory of value. While within social science there have been some theoretical attempts to surpass this dichotomy[2], community economies can be seen as highly informative for these attempts, as they not only theorise, but also practice given value forms. Community economies insist in their practice on an idea of value, which would better grasp the social element inherent in economic activity. This social element of value is not reducible to either subjective notions nor mere labour time.

---

2 Some theorists refer to 'real value', implying that there is some significant quality which should be attached to the capitalist conception of value (e.g. Kallis 2018). Others have argued that despite being quantifiable and subject to calculation, value is deeply embedded in social relations (e.g. Laamanen 2017, 3), and thereby fundamentally a comparative concept (Graeber 2013, 226).

2 – The conception of value in community economies

The task is then to explicate a theory of value from the basis of the conception embodied in practices of community economies. Community economies should be understood as economic in the sense that there is some facilitation of exchange or organisation of resources. Further, there has to be some sufficiently shared value conception. This conception can be implicit as well as explicit, yet it will be enacted in the practices of the system. The unique form of *economic value*, not accepting the mainstream economic way to draw the distinction between economic and non-economic, is one of the key components making community economies stand as a distinct category.

Below, I will sketch the key aspects of an alternative (community economy) conception of value as expressed in timebanking. 'Alternative' should be understood here in the sense of deviating from the hegemonic economics narrative, rather than as marginal: the conception can be widely enacted in everyday social life, yet discursively marginalised. The analysis will be based on a reading of key materials introducing timebanking. This comprises of, first, books and reports explaining the concept and ideology. Second, different kinds of booklets, internet publications and info leaflets are used. Third, this body of texts is complemented with interviews of some long-term timebank developers. These interviews are not systematically analysed within this chapter, but rather were used as a basis on which to form a preliminary understanding of the issue[3].

The purpose of the analysis is then to use existing material to scrutinise a conception of value within practices of alternative economies which could extend to inform the purposes of the welfare state. The conception of value is presented in terms of what is unique in it. Therefore, it includes no separate category for use-value in general: the obvious fact that people seek services because these services are useful for them.

---

[3] The interview material is used more systematically in Eskelinen 2018.

Proper recognition of the core economy
Timebanks challenge the mainstream conceptions of value by insisting that these conceptions fail to properly recognise the *value of all inputs*. In other words, only inputs which directly turn into a form with market value (commodified) are currently recognised as economically valuable. This leaves unrecognised not only subjectively valued noncommodified things but also the very basis of production and societal continuity. Indeed, a key aspect of the self-understood mission of community economies is to make visible 'the core economy', referring to the indispensable but often invisible acts of reproduction: nurturing, daily work around the household and the community. A further implication of the concept is that these activities are an essential part and basis of the economy rather than a set of fringe activities or non-productive activities (Cahn 2009; Stephens et al. 2008; Boyle et al. 2010; Cahn 2009; Coote 2010).

The undervaluation of core economy was particularly accentuated and institutionalised in the traditional gendered division of labour, which assumed females to be responsible for the 'reproductive' tasks, while males were expected to assume the 'productive' tasks. Within this interdependent division of labour, only men were recognised as producing value – and thereby rewarded with monetary compensation. This disproportionate pressure on women to focus on the 'reproductive', and its simultaneous gross undervaluation, has not ceased to exist. The conception of value highlighting the importance of 'the core economy' challenges exactly the idea that the 'reproductive' and the 'productive' could be separated along the lines of what creates and what consumes value. This is in contrast with the hegemonic economic theory which, while accepting that there is a given private sphere, has considerable difficulties in recognising any kind of economic value to be produced by this sphere (family, community). Part of the reorganisation of these categories is to properly recognise the category of community.

2 – The conception of value in community economies

The core economy is sometimes metaphorically called the 'operating system' of the more visible capitalist economy: one tends to ignore its importance, until it is in disrepair (Cahn 2004, 53–55). This refers both to its importance and universality: indeed the hidden economic activities *'everywhere* abound' (Gibson-Graham 2006b).[4] Yet the core economy is not *only* an 'operating system', but it is valuable independently of whatever might 'operate on it'. Community economies see their task as not only to make the core economy visible, but also to nurture it. Pushing for recognition for the core economy by noting its necessity for other economic functions should not lead to seeing it as only *instrumental* in producing the mainstream economic relations and institutions. It is quite a different matter to say that the core economy is vital for social well-being than to say that it is needed for the mainstream economy to function. Clearly, part of the conception of value indicated by the notion of the core economy is that it comes prior to other forms of economy and is valuable as such.

Empowerment
A major difference between the mainstream conceptions of value and the community economies' conception is that the latter insists on the *empowering* function of participation in economic exchange. Mainstream economic thought clearly shows no interest in any notion of empowerment, as this kind of 'psychology' is beyond its scope. Within this way of thinking, goods (which can be tangibles or services) exist in the market and might be subject to more or less demand, but no attention is paid to people's self-esteem or the social relations of the producer or to the effects participating in the economic process might have. The value of goods is seen to derive solely from the fact that someone desires them, in other

---

4   See also Gibson-Graham (2006b) and Mies and Bennholdt-Thomsen (1999), expressing similar kinds of ideas about the marginalisation of reproductive activities and their value as enabling all other economic activity.

words from the individual preferences.

The community economies' reversal of this approach typically comes in the form of concepts such as 'skill' or 'potential'. Timebankers insist that *nobody* is devoid of valuable skills, as everyone can contribute somehow to the community. These skills just need to be properly identified, and indeed helping others to identify this potential significantly contributes to what makes the economic process valuable. A constantly used formulation is that 'people should be recognised as assets' (Boyle et al. 2010) in contrast to treating them as expenses[5].

The idea of universal possession of valuable skills (which only sometimes need to be identified as they have become hidden by the functions of capitalist society) has several highly important implications. First, it lays the ground on perhaps the strongest normative stand within these community economies: the insistence on equality. If everyone has valuable skills, it is pointless to emphasise personal differences in quantifiable productivity. Second, it becomes equally pointless to say that some people 'feed' others, in other words produce value that is consumed by others. While any community will need some division of labour, timebanks emphasise that the capacity to contribute to the community excludes no-one, and therefore recognition as equally valuable contributors is in the heart of the practice. Third, this leads further to the empowering role of contribution: the proper identification of skills and ability to contribute can indeed be empowering through enforcing the notions of participation and belonging. While this kind of recognition is typical for social policy or social work, the explicit point in timebanking is that this is also a function of a good economy.

---

[5] Yet these ideas do have a resemblance to some formulations of the labour theory of value. Especially Marx' notion of 'living labour', which later becomes captured in capitalist labour relations. However, nothing in the concept of living labour points to active empowerment.

2 – The conception of value in community economies

Co-production

More generally, the idea of *co-production* is central in community economies. It emphasises the need to do away with a clear distinction between the producer and the recipient: if 'recipients' are involved in the production of a service, the service tends to be of better quality. Whereas tangible goods are first produced and then, separately from the production process, merely handed over to the consumer, in co-production, both the 'producer' and the 'recipient', and the 'productive process' and 'consumption' are inseparable. The notion that production and use are intertwined, has sometimes been made by using the term 'produsage' (Bruns 2007).

Yet co-production is not merely a technical notion on the need to surpass categories, but also a more general notion on the importance of social interaction in producing value. Services should be thought of as means to generate social wellbeing through interaction between human beings. Co-production practices are seen to contribute not only to making use of idle skills but also to rebuilding the social fabric. What makes economic activity valuable is that human beings meet, talk, and use common spaces. Therefore, notions such as 'community' should be part and parcel of what the economy is seen to consist of. Indeed, the conception of value which can be derived from timebanking incorporates notions such as combatting the evil of loneliness into the realm of economic value: the economy is fundamentally a process of social interaction, instead of merely mediation. (Seyfang 2004). This social nature of production cannot be grasped by either labour theory nor subjective theory of value, both of which see the lone producer or the lone consumer as a sufficient construction to represent the economic agent.

The production of services should not be seen as only a field for highly specialised professionals. Rather, to some extent, everyone should be recognised as an expert on their own life and surroundings, even if obvious differences between professions exits. If services are informed by the mainstream value model, it appears rational to organise them in highly specialised large units to benefit from economies of scale. The coproduction model completely reverses this idea, arguing that better services are created out of value produced on the community-level,[6] through the active involvement of the 'recipient'. This notion is not only a part of the community economy discourse but has revolutionary implications for the production of public services as well (Boyle and Harris 2009; Parks et al. 1981; on the effectiveness of coproduction in healthcare, see Boyle and Bird 2014; Lasker and Collom 2011).

Trust
A theory of value based on social interaction should take the virtues of the community as a starting point. Yet, community economies seek to push this even further. Such economic communities are not just any communities, but they are communities which are formed around a purpose. The embedded understanding of the economic practice is that it ought to create and sustain spaces for deliberation, political processes, and collective learning. Community economies have given shared values and promote social practices on the basis of these values.

This has implications for the given notion of generalised social trust. Based on social interaction, trust is not merely borne out of given transparent 'rules of the game'. Rather, trust is based on participation and attachment. It is not created by the stability of the system but rather negotiating its future. This is what almost all economic theories are quick to miss. Certainly, all tools and subjects of action are transformed by the very process in which they get involved (Stavrides 2016). This holds true for timebanking too, where the procedures of exchange emerge from the economic process and evolve within it.

---

6   On the significance of distance, see Stavrides 2016, 260.

2 – The conception of value in community economies

Community economies should be seen therefore as *processes* rather than *institutions*.

Trust-building is fundamentally a function of qualities of social interaction. Upholding a given identity or an expected kind of personality associated with the members of a given community can itself be trust-enhancing. For example, one timebank member argued the benefits of timebank to include, for example, that 'you tend to feel more secure asking for childcare through the timebank, having a timebank member there, instead of having just anyone'.[7] The sense of community implies a sense of belonging. Typically, belonging to the same scheme creates a psychological bond between people. Community economy schemes are often described as having the feeling of an extended family (North 2007).

The notion of extending mutual trust is well aligned with (or is a way to express) the points on empowerment and interaction mentioned above: trust within a group is generated by creating a sense of belonging. Interestingly, several timebank activists emphasise trust as an ideal, as exemplified by the title of a timebanking blog *Trust is the Only Currency*[8].

Democratic dynamism
As a last point, the conception of value in community economies resists fixed ideas of value. Therefore, it needs to be emphasised that part of this value conception is a given dynamism: community economies are venues of learning and experimentation, in which the system develops through trial and error, conflict-solving, and other microdemocratic procedures. A central aspect of the idea of value is therefore openness to new value forms. It is naturally a challenge to explicate a value conception while maintaining this openness: as a point of self-criticism, to some extent, the discussion above risks describing the community economy value

---

7   Quote from a Helsinki timebank member survey carried out by the author.
8   http://trustcurrency.blogspot.com/

form as ontologically fixed.

The difference between processes and institutions also emphasises the contrast between community economies and the capitalist mainstream. Again, trust as participation is different from trust as stability. A similar point can be noted in relation to dynamism. While capitalist dynamism is thought to derive from profit-seeking and competition between individuals, with all implied inegalitarianism, the dynamism of the community economies is the quality of systems to be open to democratic change, reaction and reflection, in other words thinking and learning together.

Welfare state and value diffusion
Next, I will turn to questions of how the conception of value in community economies can resonate with the welfare state ethos. As noted in the introduction of this book, this implies two separate questions:

1. How could the welfare state protect the abilities of community economies to operate – in this case, to sustain their value form?; and

2. To what extent can welfare states assume the value conception of community economies?

The distinction between the welfare state ethos and institutions is crucial. The welfare state as an ideal; and as a practice, should be kept clearly separate.

As for the first, a key concept organising the discussion has been 'the partner state', as, again, mentioned in the introduction of this book. When it comes to the value form, the partner state assumes a new function: that is to say the state apparatus could aim at protecting community economy ideas and practices from capitalist expansion. As capitalism expands, it transforms ever new aspects of social life into commodities, or functions in assisting capitalist value creation.

A further step is to ask: What aspects of the welfare state are in line with the value model of community economies described above? And as an accessory question: Could the existing welfare state further assume this value model as part of its functions to produce and deliver services? It is not fully clear, how the welfare state should be interpreted in this context. To some extent, welfare states, as we know them, lean heavily on a 'commodified sphere', and even push forward new frontiers of hypercommodification in an attempt to finance the welfare institutions. This function necessarily leans on the mainstream economics conception of value in which the welfare state is seen as merely a vehicle of redistribution. On the other hand, welfare states clearly have a role in maintaining commons through the governance over public goods relevant to the well-being and health of a given population, such as health and education, as long as the governance is sufficiently participatory. Further, welfare state institutions are (at least ideally) human-made and democratically planned structures which uphold a strongly egalitarian and social rights-based conception of the distribution of services.

To some extent the community economies' value conception is an explicit attempt to rival the welfare capitalist model as we know it, so the two value conceptions can be seen as somewhat conflictual. However, as noted, the welfare state *in itself* is a highly contested terrain. For these reasons it needs to be analysed, what kinds of ideas of values are *inherent* in welfare state institutions, what are *possible*, and what are *impossible*. This will enable analysing how far can welfare states be pushed in the way of the community economies' value conception.

Yet what needs to be kept in mind as a critical point is, that any activity is potentially vulnerable to commodification. This includes several aspects of the conception of value outlined above. The downside of the fact that 'the economic' and 'the social' are not ontologically separate is, that many social and emotional functions can become commodities. Affects, social relations, and generally 'the social factor' can be turned into new spheres of capitalist accumulation. So 'value diffusion' should be understood as value attached to practices which are distinctly anti-capitalist, and the ideal welfare state as a mechanism protecting diverse value conceptions.

Conceptions of value within the welfare state
I will turn next to debating what ideas and practices associated with the welfare state resonate with the conception of value discussed above. In line with the distinction made in the introductory chapter, my focus here is on the welfare state ethos, rather than the current manifesting forms. It is so that this ethos can be seen to entail ideas resembling the community economy approach more than the currently existing systems of governance.

Firstly, the notion of *trust* is clearly part of the welfare state tradition. Generalised social trust or general trust within a society, which economists prefer to call 'social capital' is often used to explain the success of economies with generous welfare systems (Halpern 2010; Whiteley 2000; World Bank 1998). While such findings as clear correlations between trust towards strangers and the economic conditions can indeed be shown, social capital tends to emerge in economics as a category for everything which cannot be explained by the traditional means of economics. This confirms how such economics is devoid of means to develop a theory on trust.

Sometimes the concept of 'endogenous growth' is used to refer to the totality including 'investments' targeted at the social fabric that reproduces and generates social capital: education being the typical example. Together with low income disparities and the good governance of basic institutions such investments foster a sense of mutual trust and secure social cohesion. It is indeed possible to discern the 'virtuous circle' of the welfare state consisting of an entanglement of strictly economic value and social goods as a single social-economic project (Hagfors et al. 2014).

Secondly, the idea of recognition can be discerned in the welfare state tradition, even if not as an economic quality. It has sometimes appeared in the form of the notion of 'talent reserve', which refers to the necessity of egalitarian education to avoid socio-economic disparities leading to wasted talents in the lack of opportunities to develop them. The tradition has also involved some notions of 'extended community', such as referring to the welfare state as the 'people's home'. Some cash transfer schemes can be seen as mechanisms for recognising everyone's input and value as human beings. For instance, certain family allowances that allow parents to take care of children at home can be seen to come close to the recognition of the core economy. Future universal recognition might take place through non-conditional transfer schemes in terms of universal basic income. In essence, one argument often made in support for universal basic income is that it would recognise the social contribution of all individuals.

Thirdly, the reproductive is seen to depend on the productive. Currently, this hierarchical order of value creation is quite central to welfare state thought; being inscribed in the very notion of the coexistence of the commodified and decommodified spheres. While reproduction is to some extent supported, the commodified sphere is seen as 'buying' the operational space for the decommodified sphere. In order to reflect the community economy conception, there would have to be a recognition of the reproductive sphere as equally or more value-creating. Fortunately, the welfare state tradition, using the notion of 'the virtuous circle', could accommodate this kind of idea.

It appears that co-production (of public services) can be integrated into the welfare state tradition if there is political will to do so. Evidently, such ideas already exist within the current discussion about organising public services, even if the wider trend is towards the commodification of services and to economies of scale. It is an open question, which also invites legitimate scepticism: *To what extent will the co-production approach permeate service provision?* The answer requires transcending several binary categorisations, such as producer/recipient, producer/product, or professional/nonprofessional – yet there is nothing inherent in the welfare state tradition, which would form an unsurmountable obstacle to this.

Of course, it is a difficult matter to change welfare state organisations, and to attempt to intermingle public functions with community economies. The major obstacles stem from path dependency and the deeply assumed preference for centralisation, which have long permeated welfare state practices. Ideas like the 'virtuous circle' and realising the potential from a talent pool within a community ultimately have leaned on increased production and hierarchical governance, even if this need not necessarily be the case.

Because of these ingrained tendencies, there is a need to find concrete examples of diffusing the alternative economy value conception. One suggestion in this direction was the call to extend the Helsinki timebank's 'time tax' into allowing municipal tax payments. This initiative was put forward when when the Finnish tax administration declared timebanks to be tax liable (Eskelinen et al. 2017). Taxation on a euro equivalent value was strongly opposed, as timebanks see their time-based currency, materialising the ethos of everyone's time being worth the same, to be not convertible to capitalist money.

The proposal was to use the timebank's platform to implement municipal taxation in time currency. Already now, in order to maintain its 'infrastructure', the timebank collects a small levy (in time) on each transaction. This levy could be used to pay the municipality of Helsinki where the timebank is based, if the municipality would open a timebank account to receive such payments. According to the proposition, the municipal account, in which time taxes accumulate, could be used by community-level municipal service providers (community centres, day care centres, parks, etc). While in a timebank no-one is obliged to provide a service, this municipal account would practically be used to reward (in time currency) people for volunteering in community-level service provision. A further function of the 'time tax' would be to challenge the category of 'work' through the official semi-economic recognition of the value of community engagement.

This suggestion serves as an example of recognising the virtues of the welfare state while pushing the community economy conception of value within the municipalities. More generally, the 'municipal tovi tax' would imply a) recognising timebanks as contributing to the community; b) diffusing the commons values into the realm of municipal services; and c) recognising the existing internal time tax model as a legitimate system of self-governance.[9]

A further issue is, if in addition to transforming public service provision this value conception could inform relations in the sphere currently referred as to 'the market'. Part of the community economy value conception is to cast the user-producer instead of the consumer as the protagonist, which opens more diverse economic subjectivities. While the matter is contested, some optimistic theorists do argue that there is a general 'move towards commons format' (Bauwens and Ramos 2018) taking place, and that this would eventually define future forms of the economy. An often noted feature of this shift is a move from possession to access, and while the latter does not automatically guarantee community economy virtues to permeate the economy, it would perhaps more easily allow this to take place. Further, some scholars expect to see a turn into 'ethical values' in the broader market, as production tends towards the production of social goods instead of tangibles in the current market (Arvidsson and Peitersen 2016).

---

9   For further practical ideas on municipalities and commons, see Ramos 2016.

Conclusions: diffusion and its limitations

The relation between the community economy value conception and the welfare state is by no means stable. This is both because of the potentially evolving nature of community economies and the ongoing political struggles over welfare states. For this reason, the welfare state should be approached both as an ideal ('ethos') and as a really existing system ('institution'). From the institutional perspective, it is possible to consider, how far could the welfare state ideally go in incorporating and assisting the community economy value conception (keeping in mind that inaction from the state will always be the preference of some community economy organisers). On the other hand, the welfare state can be seen as an ideal as well, or as a (constantly evolving) reminder of the social and egalitarian aspects of value.

While it is important to analyse the capacity of welfare states to be informed by the value conception from the community economies, it needs to be noted that to some extent the value form of the community economies is bound to the immediate community. Therefore, at least to some extent it will not be institutionalised outside the community level, even though some commons activists note that commons need to be seen as having a unique form of upscaling (Helfrich 2013, 14–15). 'Scaling up' (Utting 2015) would then potentially imply diminished social value, as systems reach such a large scale that they no longer facilitate community-level interaction where people know each other personally.

For example, a major question is, whether the welfare state is able to recognise the generation of trust as within its mission. Within many social services the generation of trust and sense of participation can be quite explicit goals, yet economically, the capitalist conception of value situates trust as 'exogenous' to the theory of value. It is plausible that the community economy conception of value could demonstrate ideas on what economic value fundamentally consists of to influence welfare state praxis in

2 – The conception of value in community economies

the future. Another key issue is, whether trust is seen as primarily generated by quality institutions (see Ingham 2004 on 'assigned trust'), or by participatory virtues.

Any diffusion of the community economy conception of economic value to the welfare state is unlikely to happen in the form of a sudden transformation of state governance. Rather, this change could most plausibly take place on the operational level of community economies, namely local or municipal levels. A number of services provided by municipalities already operate as forms of commons, and they could be easily reorganised so as to reflect the above-mentioned values of core economy, empowerment, co-production, trust, and democratic dynamism. Yet a further and more complex issue is how to transfer this conception of value to the sphere of the economic from the sphere of non-economic services.

Practically, government policies are substantially informed by some value conception. While a value conception is not explicit or conscious, it largely dictates, what is seen as worth doing. A labour-oriented value conception will lead to attempts to maximise commodified labour and to interpret a high labour force participation rate as the key indicator of success. It will also lead to social policy solutions that consider participation in the labour market as a goal in its own right. Demand-based conception will lead to maximising market spaces and market transactions, creating a thorough marketisation of large spheres of life. In terms of social services, a demand-based value conception sees always more value in services which have been acquired by the means of market choices, rather than for instance political engagement. Thus, the result will easily be a hypercommodified reality.

Based on timebanking, as an illuminating example of the community economy value conception, I have argued that included in this conception are five specific spheres of value in addition to the general use-value of services: recognition of the core economy, empowerment, co-production, trust, and democratic dynamism. These ideas herald a significant move forward from the ostensibly exhaustive dichotomy in the economic literature, which is comprised of labour and subjective theories of value. The conception of value sketched here is a challenge to economic thought at large, as it grounds value in a way which is incompatible with major economic theories. This conception is particularly important as it insists on value being based on human interaction and recognition. Furthermore, the community economy value concept should be treated as a call to recognise and protect the unique spaces of community economy. As social interaction, culture and care; which are beholden to human interaction, are often threatened with commodification, they are bolstered in the demands to be handled outside the sphere of capitalism by the existence of community economies.

Seeing these value conceptions as mutually exclusive easily leads to the perception that the only future choices for welfare states are productivism or marketisation. Clearly, political manoeuvres dismantling the welfare state are often made in the name of saving it, in reference to the need to increase the general employment level by disciplining the workforce, or to increase economic transactions by privatising public services. That these kinds of policies can be derived from the mainstream value conceptions as pro-welfare state policies, shows the high importance of questioning such value conceptions and suggesting more sustainable alternatives.

The value conception of the community economies should be understood as *reminding* the welfare state of its normative basis, which is not merely about redistributing money and organising services. For instance, public services should always involve an element of local and democratic control. Most aspects of the community economies' conception of value could be accommodated within the welfare state tradition: co-production and participatory approaches in public services could expand, categories of productive/reproductive and professional/volunteer could be reconsidered, and trust could be seen as a participatory virtue. Finally, the welfare state can also intermingle its functions with community economies, allowing itself to learn from these systems and more deeply incorporate their logic of operation into itself. The key question is then if the welfare state institutions are able to recognise this approach not only as instrumental or complementary to value production, but as the very definition of value. This will not happen without political struggle turning the tide.

3
Diverse work practices and the role of welfare institutions

Tuuli Hirvilammi & Maria Joutsenvirta

Cultivating community economies is an enormous endeavour requiring active efforts and the competent employment of committed members. Even though these efforts are not always monetarily rewarded or officially recognised as 'work', they are indispensable for building sustainable economies. This typical situation is the starting point of this chapter that focuses on the tension between work, as understood within community economies, and the currently hegemonic ideas and norms of employment. How can people devote their agency and time to constructing community economies, when they should also be able to survive in a capitalist economy, perhaps being pushed to full-time wage labour by disciplining authorities?

Research on community economies emphasises the importance of seeing the variety of conceptualisations of 'labour' and 'work' and ways to perform it. Besides waged labour, alternative paid and unpaid labour as well as work for welfare (subsidised work or conditional work that is done in order to receive social benefits) play essential roles (Gibson-Graham and Roelvink 2011). However, this variety of work forms is undermined in contemporary capitalist welfare states as they rely on the idea and norm of full-time waged labour and productivism (e.g. Fitzpatrick and Cahill 2002). Welfare institutions continue to make a clear distinction between unpaid reproductive work and paid productive work and give recognition mainly to the latter, thus failing to adequately value socially and economically essential work done in communities and households. This shortcoming is visible in the strictly conditional social allowances and activation policies in Nordic welfare states (e.g. Johansson 2001). Activation policies and welfare institutions in general largely ignore and discourage unpaid work done in community economies as this form of work does not create monetary economic value. This policy derives from the conventional models of economics and a narrow conception of economically valuable relations and exchanges (Eisler 2007; Gibson-Graham 2008; Halpern 2010; Raworth 2018). We can therefore assume that community economies and the associated diverse work practices that question the premises of welfare institutions can face challenges in current Nordic welfare states.

In this chapter,[10] we will look at the practical ramifications of norms and policies by welfare institutions regarding the work practices within the community economies. As Gritzas and Kavoulakos (2016, 924) have acknowledged, community economic spaces are always constrained by the existing power relations that manifest in concrete places and times. The given constraints and contradictions imply different degrees of alterity and possibility of their achieving post-capitalist futures. To examine the potential of community economies in welfare states and to identify possible institutional challenges, we studied two Finnish community

---

10   The empirical study is part of the research project ECOSOS 'Contribution of Social Work and Systems of Income Security to the Ecosocial Transformation of Society' at the University of Jyväskylä, led by professor Aila-Leena Matthies and funded by the Academy of Finland for the years 2015-2019 (285868). The first author was involved in this research project and acknowledges the financial support of the Academy of Finland.

economies: an organic food cooperative and an autonomous social centre with an art exhibition space. The first author visited these sites, observed their everyday practices, collected documentary material and conducted interviews in 2017. During the interviews, the participants were asked to describe the background of their initiative, typical activities and resources, organisation structures and networks, and personal motivations. Specific questions focused on the relationships with public authorities and possible institutional challenges.

The aim of this chapter is to provide insight on the present tensions between welfare institutions and the diverse work practices of community economies. Moreover, it helps to recognise measures through which welfare institutions might support a broader conception of work. We explore, how people can be active in unpaid alternatives when they should also be able to sustain themselves. We identify a large variety of work forms in these two organisations drawing on the diverse economy framing by Gibson-Graham (2008; see also Introduction) and see how welfare institutions influence organising the work.

We argue that a broader conception of work and enabling welfare institutions could have important roles in supporting and giving value to the full range of economic practices, which include not only monetarily rewarded labour but also alternative paid and unpaid work. The different aims and practices between community economies and activation policies in Nordic welfare states provide a fruitful context for analysing the tension between diverse work within community economies, and the currently hegemonic ideas of 'work' and 'labour'.

From a narrow conception of labour to diverse work practices
Our proposition is that a broad conceptualisation and implementation of work creates possibilities for community economies and less exploitative conditions of employment in both a social and ecological sense. It does so by making visible

and giving value not only to such human agency and occupation that can be more meaningful and fulfilling than conventional salaried labour but also to a wide range of economic relations and exchanges.

One way to expand the understanding of work is the analytical distinction between the concepts of 'labour' and 'work'. In describing the general human conditions, Hannah Arendt (2013, original 1958) distinguishes three forms of practical activities: labour, work and action. For her, labour arises from the necessity of biological survival whereas work is related to our need to construct human settlements, to create culture and to produce artefacts. Action, in turn, takes place in relation to other human beings, in communal and political spheres. All these elements are necessary for a human life and therefore they are the basis for approaching work in community economy building.

In a similar vein and applied in the context of modern welfare states, British economist Guy Standing (2009) has argued that work and labour are not synonymous: 'not all work is labour, while not all labour is productive activity.' (Ibid., 5.) For him, work captures all positive aspects of productive, reproductive and creative activity, which gives room and respect to inaction and contemplation. Labour and salaried employment, in turn, do not leave such space.[11] In performing work, a person has agency and a sense of self-determination. Work raises the idea of occupation, a sense of calling and a lifetime of creative and dignifying work

---

11 The word 'labour' is derived from the Latin laborem, implying toil, distress and trouble. Laborare meant to do heavy onerous work. The ancient Greek word for labour, ponos, signified pain and effort, and has a similar etymological root as the Greek word for poverty, penia. So labour meant painful, onerous activity done in conditions of poverty. Labour's function is to produce marketable output or services. Those who control labour usually want to take advantage of others, and often will oppress and exploit those performing labour. Labour is also associated with 'jobs' and the 'jobholder society' as described by Hannah Arendt. In a job, a person performs 'labour'; sometimes identified as alienated activity because it is instrumental and requires the person to carry out a predetermined set of tasks. (Standing 2009, 6.)

around a self-chosen set of activities. For Standing, 'occupational citizenship' and 'occupational community' contain innate psychic value in the work and the social relations in which it takes place. They also provide a mechanism for social solidarity. An integral part of occupation is the reproductive work not only in terms of nurturing and caring, but also as involving acts of civic friendship that reproduce the community – containing thus the role of action in Arendt's categorisation. By contrast, a worker required to perform labour often lacks agency, and there is no room for these types of activities and identities. This is especially so when people do labour as alienated employees and primarily for instrumental reasons, under somebody's control. (Standing 2009, 4–14.)

Since industrialisation, western welfare systems have been influenced heavily by what can be called 'industrial citizenship', the essence of which has been the extension of social rights – entitlements and norms associated with industrial wage labour (Standing 2009, 3–5). According to Standing (2009), twentieth-century progressives made a mistake in making labour and employment the focus of social protection, regulation and redistribution. 'If you laboured for wages, you built up entitlements to sick leave, unemployment benefits, maternity leave, disability benefits and a pension.' (Standing 2009, 7.) Consequently, unpaid reproductive work had become unproductive and had disappeared altogether from public view, censuses and labour statistics (Standing 2009, 5). The 'invisible' work does not then contribute to GDP growth that the welfare institutions depend on (see Chapter 1).

The criticism of capitalist welfare models for their incapacity to recognise necessary reproductive and unpaid work is one of the starting points in the community economy literature. A key premise of this discussion is the need to extend the narrow types of economic relations in which surplus value is produced, appropriated and distributed on the basis of waged labour and production for the market and mainstream market finance modes

(Gibson-Graham 2010; see also Mazzucato 2018). The framing of diverse economies broadens the conception of work and other key aspects of economy. It emphasises the role of different modes of economic organisation and different ways of performing and remunerating labour – not only waged and salaried labour, but also alternatively paid labour and unpaid labour (Gibson-Graham and Roelvink 2011, 29). In any case, non-market transactions and unpaid household work (both by definition non-capitalist) have been estimated to constitute close to or as much as half of economic activity in both rich and poor countries – if approached from the perspective of their potential market value (Ironmonger 1996; Gibson-Graham 2008).

Theorising on diverse forms of work in community economy literature (including and mixing both concepts of 'labour' and 'work') allows consideration of diverse production spaces and processes that extend our understanding of how and where value is produced (see also Chapter 2). Since J.K. Gibson-Graham view the economy as referring to all practices that allow us to survive and care for each other and the earth, they also endorse diverse forms of work. Diverse economic framing identifies alternative paid labour and unpaid work practices that might be pursued by households, communities and civic institutions to generate well-being for people and the planet. Diverse types of work provide not just necessary material well-being but also social, community, spiritual, physical, and environmental well-being (Gibson-Graham et al. 2017; see also Hirvilammi and Helne 2014). Acknowledging all the positive aspects of work done within community economies requires a broad conceptualisation of work, which is why below we will use the concept of work to cover a whole spectrum of necessary practices to organize, govern and sustain community economies.

Activation policies in Nordic welfare states
Welfare states are characterised by state-funded and state-organised

welfare systems that aim to guarantee social protection for all their citizens. When looking at the concrete forms and legislation of welfare states, full employment and self-support through wage labour have always been seen as the priorities for welfare and as preconditions for maintaining the welfare systems and thereby as important political goals – despite the idealistic prominence on decommodification (e.g. Esping-Andersen 1990.) Consequently, work incentives and work obligations have played significant roles in Nordic welfare states (Johansson 2001). Social benefits are mostly directed at people who are outside the labour market due to illness, unemployment or disability, for example. A high employment rate is seen as necessary, not only for tax revenues, but also for high wellbeing outcomes. The guiding belief in social policy is that it should always be more beneficial to work than to live on benefits.

The incentives and obligations for citizens to be employed have become even stricter since the emergence of the 'activation paradigm' in the 1990s. For example, Finland during this era introduced new work incentives in the unemployment insurance and social assistance systems in order to stimulate high labour-market participation (Johansson 2001). Unemployed people became objects of activation measures: they had to report more often to the Public Employment Office, actively seek jobs and accept work offers. Since 2001, the long-term recipients of unemployment benefits have been obliged to have an 'activation plan' in which the officers from the 'Public employment and business service' and social workers together with the job seeker agree to the most efficient pathways towards employment (Minas et al. 2018).

Due to the activation paradigm, the focus of social policies in Nordic welfare states has shifted from welfare to workfare (e.g. Johansson 2001) – or 'labourfare', if the above distinction between work and labour is followed. In practice, welfare systems aim to encourage welfare recipients to seek routes to employment with the help of various activation programs, such as supported employment, work trials and wage allowances. On other occasions, job seekers must meet the requirements of activation policies by taking part in work trials provided by public, private or third sector actors, for example. When taking part in these programs, the unemployed person is entitled to unemployment benefit and a small daily allowance.

Sanctions and conditionality have become central parts of social security. When unemployed people have to participate in some activation programme to be entitled to unemployment benefit, they are obliged to work in exchange for the social benefit, not in exchange for better income or a decent salary. The possibilities of refusing to participate in a directed programme have been curtailed, and authorities have been granted more sanctioning possibilities. Even though the Finnish constitution guarantees social protection for all, the minimum level, last-resort social assistance has been made more conditional. Since 1996, the Finnish authorities have had the right to reduce the level of social assistance by 20 percent if a recipient refuses to participate in an offered activation measure, and 40 percent on the second refusal. (See Minas et al. 2018; Johansson 2001.)

For the purposes of our study, it is important to note how these activation policies are built on the narrow conception of full-time paid labour. The work done in various types of community economies is not always acknowledged as an activity that should be accounted for by the welfare system. For instance, if unemployment benefits claimants are actively involved in local communities or occupied with taking care of ill family members, both of which are important forms of occupational citizenship (Standing 2009) or caring for each other and the earth (Gibson-Graham et al. 2017), they are not entitled to unemployment benefits. Active volunteering can violate the norm that all registered job seekers have to be available for full-time jobs.

Two case studies: Oma Maa and Hirvitalo

Below, we will describe the analysis of work practices in two established community economies in Finland: the food cooperative Oma Maa and the Pispala Contemporary Art Center informally called Hirvitalo. They are valuable subjects of study active in different fields, food and art, but they share similar ethical guidelines and missions of a more participatively democratic and sustainable society. Thus, they enable an investigation of a variety of practices that grow in the 'hidden neverland' (Gritzas and Kavoulakos 2016) of the Finnish welfare state.

The first case, Oma Maa ('Our soil'/'Our land'), is an organic food cooperative founded during 2009 in an old farm with a tradition of organic farming, located 30 km outside of Helsinki. Oma Maa assumes a community-supported agriculture approach[12] characterised by short distances between producers and consumers and a focus on community building, thus acting as a counterforce to commercial organic food production. The mission of Oma Maa is to develop food production in which the means of production are commonly owned by its members. The future vision is a completely self-reliant and fossil-free farm. The producer-members of the co-operative produce the food at the farm and deliver it to the consumer-members. At the time of data collection, there were less than 10 producer-members, who were actively taking responsibility for farming, preparation of food products, food delivery and a lunch café. Around 60 consumer-members of the cooperative paid a monthly fee which allows them to collect their weekly food bags directly from the farm, or from the café that the cooperative also runs in Helsinki. The lunch café offers a vegan lunch every weekday in a commercially rented

---

12   See e.g. https://www.ifoam.bio/en/community-supported-agriculture-csa

space from the private market[13]. The funding of the cooperative is mainly based on membership fees and food bag sales in addition to some occasional agricultural subsidies.

Hirvitalo – Pispala Contemporary Art Center, is located in a lively and artistic neighbourhood Pispala, in Tampere, Finland. Hirvitalo ('Moose house', named after the street it is on Hirvikatu – meaning Moose Street in Finnish) was founded in 2006 by a small group of artists who were looking for a space for art exhibitions and social gatherings. After the small group of culture activists initially discovered the empty old wooden house, they were able to rent the house from the city of Tampere at a very reduced rent (or at peppercorn rent). Nowadays, Hirvitalo is run by the Pispala Culture Association that was founded to stimulate the cultural activities of Hirvitalo and to enrich various kinds of artistic and cultural events in the local community. Hirvitalo is an alternative non-capitalist cultural space that is against a monocultural society. It is open to all and for all. It has space for exhibitions, installations and it hosts many meetings and various cultural projects. The house is open a minimum five days a week, five hours a day. A 'community kitchen' serves vegan food almost every Saturday, a sauna is heated once a week and outdoor events are organised during the summertime. Everybody is welcome to come in and use the carpentry workshop or the band rehearsal space, or to have a cup of coffee and chat with others. Only occasional grants and member fees of the association have been used to fund the costs of Hirvitalo and the events that occurred there[14].

---

13   At the time of the interview, the cooperative ran a lunch café in Helsinki but since then it has finished serving lunch every day. The space is still used for sharing food bags and for organizing events.

14   After the data gathering, the Pispala Culture Association received a 27 000 euro grant for art exhibitions and gallery support from the Kone Foundation (https://koneensaatio.fi/en/grants/tuetut/2017-2/annual-funding-round-arts-8-dec-2017/).

3 – Diverse work practices

Diversity in work practices

In Oma Maa, work tasks derive from the necessities of cultivation and food distribution. It is necessary that land is cultivated, and someone needs to take care of plowing, fertilising, sowing, weeding, harvesting, animal husbandry etc. A large number of working hours are also needed for baking bread for the weekly food bags and for producing other food products like falafel balls and bags of spelt flour. At the time of the interviews, the lunch for the café was produced daily, and someone also had to bake cakes, make coffee and wash the dishes. In addition, some members are responsible for building a new greenhouse and transporting the food bags from the farm to Helsinki. Web pages and social media updates need to be done, as well as the administration of the cooperative, such as invoices, billing, membership fees and the registration of new members. Also, the tasks and division of responsibilities need to be managed and discussed to keep all things running. Since the number of active members is less than ten, the most active producer-members work long days. In addition, some consumer-members take voluntarily part in distributing the food bags and helping in the farm during the high season.

Various efforts in Hirvitalo relate to maintenance and organisational chores of different kinds. First of all, at least one person, a gallerist, is needed to keep the doors open five days a week, to work with visiting artists and look after the art exhibition. Their tasks also include cleaning the house and heating it with wood during the winter months. The community kitchen is organised on Saturdays, only if there is someone to cook the food, and the sauna is heated whenever there is a common sauna evening. Upcoming art exhibitions need to be curated and web pages updated. Someone always has to take care of book keeping and fund raising, as well as other formal and legal responsibilities. In practice, the board members of the association and other active and regular visitors share the tasks. Many of the original members are still involved and visit Hirvitalo on a regular basis. Active participants are the most important resource of Hirvitalo: it is a space where anything can happen, but nothing happens if people are not inspired to organise the events and be involved.

This all sounds similar to many other small companies or organisations. However, there is one significant feature that makes these diverse work practices different from more mainstream entrepreneurship: all this necessary work is mainly non-salaried and non-monetized. Due to low financial resources of these organisations, members do a large part of the work without monetary rewards. For example, the Oma Maa producer-members work without monetary compensation, except for three farmers who have been paid during the summer months. Since the cooperative is not able to pay more salaries, some active members are officially unemployed and live with the help of unemployment benefits. Because many active members have to do paid work elsewhere to make their ends meet, they cannot devote their working time to the development of the co-op. This is a big challenge for the further development of this alternative form of economy, and one which can lead to a vicious cycle: as long as the members are not able to invest enough time and effort for the organizational development, the organisations cannot grow big enough to survive financially. Only if all the necessary work was done, could they gain a sufficiently stable position. Similar challenges in providing a sufficient living wage, and the demand to navigate diverse economies in order to survive have been experienced by small-scale social enterprises in Finland too (Houtbeckers 2018).

All of the aforementioned activities in Hirvitalo are based on voluntary work or on work done by trainees whose income is covered by the welfare state and its activation policies. Due to its limited financial resources, the Pispala Culture Association has not been able to employ any fulltime workers without state subsidies. Contrary to many more mainstream art initiatives, Hirvitalo has been developed with a very tight budget. The active members emphasise the roots of Hirvitalo being from a collective inspiration to make art and to have an alternative gallery that should be free from monetary rewards and competition. The lack of financial resources has been partly a deliberate choice. Moreover, the members prefer to be active outside the capitalist monetary economy, and they intentionally seek to oppose existing unequal power structures. The interviewees argued that the combination of large grants and a small number of paid positions could be problematic because it would threaten the equal power structure within the small community in Hirvitalo. For the sake of equality, the board of the association has decided that all activities organised by Hirvitalo will be free (only small fees can be gathered in order to cover the costs). This is important in allowing the space to be really open to everyone regardless of one's ability to pay.

Both Oma Maa and Hirvitalo enact a large variety of work practices. Active members are involved in paid work and work for welfare but also in non-monetised and non-capitalist exchanges. Reciprocal work has been utilised in the form of exchanging services. For example, some farming work at Oma Maa has been done by people from other associations who have, in exchange, been allowed to use the café space. Oma Maa is also a member of the Helsinki Timebank called Stadin Aikapankki (see Joutsenvirta 2016). Over the years of Oma Maa's activity, some members of the time bank have been working in the fields, being compensated through the time currency system. Oma Maa has then 'earned time' by renting the space and through Helsinki Timebank's own internal taxation system (see also Chapter 2). Hirvitalo activists have mutually exchanged services with other local groups without using any currency. For example, they have got help with advertising and could use a van in exchange for some other favours. Also, the practices of in-kind work are seen in exchanging the work with food. For example, the members who work at the lunch café or prepare the meal for the community kitchen can have a lunch for free. Table 1. illustrates these diverse ways of organising work in Oma Maa and Hirvitalo inspired by the examples of diverse work practices in the community economy literature (e.g. Gibson-Graham and Roelvink 2011).

	OMA MAA	HIRVITALO
Paid work	Three farmers are paid on summertime	No paid workers
Self-employed	Self-employed positions enable the participants to be engaged in Oma Maa	Self-employed positions and freelance work as an artist enable the particants to be engaged in Hirvitalo
Reciprocal work	Help from the members of other associations as an exchange for the use of the café space, experiments of using community currencies	Exchange of services with other associations (car use, advertising, coproducing events)
In-kind	People get sometimes food products when they work	People can eat for free when they prepare meal for social kitchen
Work for welfare, subsidized work	Some experiences of people sent by unemployment office, unemployed people in work trial	Always one person who is officially unemployed is doing her/his work trial in Hirvitalo, or some other forms of subsidized work is in use
Housework	Cooking, cleaning etc.	Heating the house, cooking, cleaning etc.
Unpaid work	Most of the activities and production are based on unpaid work	Unpaid work is necessary for organizing events
Self-provisioning	Food production	Gardening, growing vegetables

Table 1. The diverse ways of organizing the work tasks in Oma Maa and Hirvitalo.

3 – Diverse work practices

The diversity of work is a creative way to combine the necessary work of community economies with their members' aspirations and lifestyles. Many interviewees are critical towards conventional paid labour and prefer more autonomous and meaningful ways to be occupied. This is in line with the notion that the work in community economies is not a less desirable second choice (White and Williams 2016). Our interviewees see work in their community economy as an important element to moderate the societal focus on full-time paid labour done only for instrumental reasons and under somebody's control. The work in community economy is a transformative, but at the same time very down-to-earth, path towards reduced working time and sustainable lifestyles:

> 'I do have a very idealistic wish that it might be great if we had less paid jobs and we would have more... Like starting from the farmers that the food comes closer and it would be cheaper and people would work less. Then they would have more time to be involved in these kinds of projects and it would be more ecological. That somehow this society requires us, it forces us to have an eight-hour workday and the salary so that you can survive. But if these kinds of projects grew and people joined, it would be my dream.' (Oma Maa 1)

The reproductive and creative work done in community economies is different from conventional and often monotonous salaried labour. For many interviewees, there seems to be a joy for creating alternative food networks or autonomous spaces outside the monocultural structures of society. Some interviewees who are self-employed in the ICT or marketing sector, for example, do unpaid work in Oma Maa or Hirvitalo to get a better balance between their professional life and transformative values. It seems that the work in Oma Maa and Hirvitalo is closely related to 'a sense of calling' (Standing 2009, 12; see also Domene 2012), identity and ideological commitments of the active members. They do not always count hours or ask for monetary rewards, but the sense of being part of the community is a key driver for being involved. Especially people who spent days at Hirvitalo or worked in the Oma Maa lunch café saw it as an important common space that can prevent isolation and loneliness of people who are lacking a full-time paid job or a work community:

> 'It was maybe some kind of social need, when I moved. I know many people here in Pispala and some of them come here occasionally. So I kind of missed – when I don't have any job or anything – this kind of social space where you can come so that you don't have to buy anything, that you can just come. It's so good that these kind of places do exist.' (Hirvitalo 3)

The relationship between community economies and the welfare institutions

Knowing that community economies are constrained by the existing power relations and state structures (Gritzas and Kavoulakos 2016), we will next take a closer look at the role of the state and examine whether welfare institutions are supporting or rather preventing the building of community economies and concomitant meaningful citizen occupation.

The impact of the welfare state, through its social security systems and activation policies, is Janus-faced. Our findings show that various norms, rules and practices have both enabling and limiting impacts on individuals and community economies. The relationship is conflicted, also for the interviewees: they emphasized freedom and autonomy from the official economy, but they were also aware of how dependent they still were on the social security systems and the norms of a labour society.

Unemployment benefits, housing benefits and social assistance can provide a necessary minimum income for those who are actively involved in communities and occupied in unpaid work. More than half of our interviewees received unemployment benefit as their main source of income. The official target of the Finnish welfare state is that all job seekers participate in formal activation programmes rather than do informal volunteering. However, because officials cannot control all jobseekers, the social security system allows unemployed people to be active in various associations. As our interviews show, unemployment benefit can be used for quite a long time without any disturbance, for developing various skills, for making art or for farming. Due to the very low level of unemployment benefits or minimum social assistance in relation to living costs in present Finnish society, unemployed people must live on a very low monetary income. Many interviewees describe their difficulties in getting by when trying to work hard to cultivate community economies. This sheds light on the paradoxical situation: the activists are fully occupied in meaningful value creating activities, but in the eyes of the welfare institutions, they are categorized as unemployed or marginalized poor people.

In addition to providing social benefits for the cultivators of community economies, some activation programmes can be beneficial for community economy building when enabling various ways for compensating the work. For example, at Hirvitalo, there is always one person in a work trial or with a wage allowance who can keep the gallery open. To be able to work at Hirvitalo, this person needs to be officially unemployed so that they have the right to participate in the activation programme organised by the employment office. During the activation programme period, the worker receives an amount of 9 euro per day over the minimum unemployment benefit. If the Pispala Culture Association meets the official requirements and employment officials have sufficient financial resources, Hirvitalo can be also entitled to a wage allowance measure, in which the state supports the association to employ a worker. The Public Employment Office has to agree with any work trial and the length of the wage allowance period. With this system, many active members of the association have been able to be employed by Hirvitalo.

However, the increasingly limiting approach of welfare institutions is also experienced by Oma Maa and Hirvitalo. For example, the possibilities for using wage allowance have been recently curtailed. According to the interviewees, the authorities have also restricted the length of work trials:

> Interviewee: 'If you try to get here for six months, for example, they would send you a refusal for the other half of the period. At least nowadays.'
>
> Researcher: 'Why, on the basis of what?'
>
> Interviewee: 'They might think that this is somehow a suspicious place for work trials because this is not a proper company that would focus on financial profit. Maybe they are skeptical of the value of this place as something that can give work experience.' (Hirvitalo 5)

This quotation hints at the narrow concept of work and productivity. The authorities do not see work done at Hirvitalo as *real* work because it does not provide a pathway to wage-labour. Even though many activation programmes are currently more related to rehabilitation and meaningful activities especially for long-term unemployed people than to a direct access to real wage-labour, the case of limiting the period of a work trial indicates that the activation policies tend to see wage-labour as a primary goal (see also Johansson 2001, 74). This again gives reason to support the argument that welfare institutions are geared towards 'industrial citizenship', whereby the normative foundation of social protection, regulation and redistribution is wage labour and full-time employment (Standing 2009). With this emphasis, the system fails to take full advantage of supporting unemployed people to be active in community economies or to encourage them in building sustainable economies and livelihoods. Moreover, if welfare institutions give a preference to accepting work trials in for-profit companies rather than in community economies or other not-for-profit sectors, the system can be (ab)used to provide free labour for maximising private, narrowly understood economic gain, rather than fostering wider societal goals and values, such as building new sustainable economic structures and strengthening social ties.

Another example of the narrow concept of work and difficulties of welfare institutions in dealing with the small-scale community economies is the case of those unemployed people who have to be *passive* in the eyes of authorities in order to get their unemployment benefits. The following quotation from one active member in Oma Maa illustrates this situation well:

> Interviewee: 'No way I would never go and tell in the unemployment office that I do something. If they asked, I would just say that I lay on the couch all day long, it would be a big mistake to tell that you do something.'
>
> Researcher: 'Why?'
>
> Interviewee: 'Well, I don't know. They have not really asked me. It must be something like five or six years ago since I have talked face-to-face with unemployment officers and they have not been interested in my situation. But it is obvious that it would be quite easy for them to see me as an entrepreneur because I am a member of the cooperative and I am sitting on the board etc.' (Oma Maa 3)

The main fear of this particular interviewee was to be categorised as an entrepreneur by employment authorities because a person who owns a company is not entitled to unemployment benefit (or at least the authorities will ask for exhaustive reports on the financial situation of the company). This can significantly reduce the incentives to be active in community economies.

Besides describing the challenges, we elaborated what an enabling partner state could look like and how to develop the system so that it would be better in line with the needs of alternative economy building. Firstly, the most reformist suggestion is to simplify the social security system. For example, it should be easier to have a half-time paid job and combine the salary with social benefits. Due to the complexity of the social benefits system, Oma Maa has for example paid full-time salaries to the farmers only for three months so that the people can then apply for unemployment benefit for the rest of the year. Since the cooperative would rather pay part-time salaries during the whole year, this is one example how the social security system influences the decisions made in these cases.

Secondly, many interviewees advocate a universal basic income that would provide necessary financial security:

> 'I think that the basic income would be a good idea, because it gives the possibility, that if you wish to live with less money and you have many ideas, you would still have that security.' (Oma Maa 4)

Basic income could also encourage people to be involved in small cooperatives and take financial risks. The implementation of basic income could allow many people who are seeking for more sustainable alternatives to reduce the amount of time spent in paid labour and substitute paid labour with other types of meaningful work (e.g. Alexander 2015).

Thirdly, the interviewees want less policies and regulation; *inaction* from the state and municipalities (see Introduction). Oma Maa and Hirvitalo are geared to build autonomous alternatives, spaces free from the capitalocentric economy and outside of state structures. Active members try to arrange the economy based on commons and commoning. They develop the practices of horizontal decision-making with weekly house meetings to govern the resources and to share power. Oma Maa tries to get rid of external funding systems such as agricultural subsidies. Hirvitalo wishes to have a long-term and cheap rental agreement with the city of Tampere so that they will be allowed to stay and create the space for a do-it-yourself (DIY) culture. Instead of regulation and formal project funding, they only wish to have basic enabling structures, a space for collective actions and the time of active members, and to be able to carry on the cultivation of community economies.

Conclusions: making the sustainability transition through diverse work and new time allocation
The diversity of work practices in the two cases of community economies relate both to the financial limits and to the personal aspirations of the active members. Work in community economies is meaningful and fulfilling to their members in many ways. It also seems to support the transition to sustainability on both the individual and societal levels (see EEA 2018).

Our findings show how employment policies and the social security system can have both enabling and hindering impacts on the possibilities to enact community economies. On the one hand, the welfare system enables by providing social benefits for those actors who are officially unemployed so that they can be active outside paid work. The community economy cases have also found creative ways to benefit from activation programmes. On the other hand, the employment policy regulations and activation policies hinder the development of community economies. This happens through limiting citizens' possibilities to voluntarily reduce one's dependence on full-time paid labour in order to become active in other forms of value creating activities and occupational identities. Because not all activities of unemployed people are acknowledged as belonging to activation programmes, the welfare system is bound up in a narrow 'labourfare' rather than a broader 'workfare' that would allow diverse practices of work.

In consumerist and Protestant work ethic-oriented Nordic welfare states peoples' self-worth is often connected to outdated, industrial-age understandings of a secure livelihood and material elements of good life. Yet at the same time, many full-time paid jobs are experienced as having no meaning and giving no fulfilment to their holders – especially in administrative, managerial and clerical roles (Graeber 2018). Despite the ongoing transition of work-life to more insecure labour positions (e.g. Standing 2009), welfare institutions are still designed on the basis of full-participation in full-time labour. The focus on labour rather than on a broader concept of work contradicts with community economies' non-monetised and alternatively paid work practices. Fixing this shortcoming is one of the key missions on our way towards institutional learning (see Chapter 1) in which the state authorities would question the overruling position of full-time salaried work and apply a wider understanding of how value is created and distributed in our changing societies.

We can conclude that the present welfare institutions are not fitted to support individually and socially important work done in community economies. Due to activation policies following 'the dictate of competitiveness', welfare states lack effective agency to guide towards occupational citizenship and diversified work practices (Standing 2009, 282–285). Current social benefits and employment policies do not sufficiently value the necessary work outside 'official employment'; the work which would not only enable citizens and households to survive but also benefit other people and the environment (Gibson-Graham et al. 2017).

However, the unpaid and alternatively paid work practices could make important day-to-day progress in supporting lifestyles that depart from the unsustainable consumption and work patterns (Gibson-Graham et al. 2017; Schor 2010; Coote and Franklin

2013). Moreover, they could have a significant role in building bottom-up solutions for meeting the governmental commitments to achieve global sustainable development goals (SDGs) by 2030 (see e.g. Folke et al. 2016). The diverse work practices could also influence the future of work in general by making it more humane, flexible and connected to real human needs rather than a motor that supports unsustainable production and consumption patterns. When ignoring the diversity of work, welfare states are at risk of missing out this transformative potential.

There is an urgent need for both economists and policy makers to seriously address climate change and other sustainability issues and transform the welfare states in an ecological direction through integrative ecosocial policies (e.g. Hirvilammi and Helne 2014; Koch and Mont 2016; Gough 2017). The present emphasis on technology, efficiency and markets keeps the conventional mechanisms for job creation in place, thereby preventing major transformations in how people gain access to work and income. To overcome this problem, the rich North should confront its commitment to economic growth by averting continued increases in the scale of consumption through trading income for time (e.g. Schor 2005; 2013; see Chapter 1) This can be done, for example, by relinquishing our 'fetish for labour productivity', i.e. the desire continually to increase the output delivered by each hour of working time (Jackson 2013). However, there are no simple formulas to re-organise work and re-write welfare policies according to what has been discussed. It is complicated by the complex ways in which different policies and habits, roles and responsibilities, and interests and institutions interact (Coote 2013). To address the need for reorganising employment and welfare policies, we propose two concrete policy proposals that might enable the welfare state to better support the broad understanding of work.

First, as an alternative for activation policies and conditional social benefits based on the notion of full-time labour, the universal basic income could provide a more fruitful basis for building sustainable forms of economies and lifestyles. With a basic income, people could have more time for meaningful work and sustainable value creation in informal economies (e.g. Fitzpatrick 2011). If a universal and unconditional basic income is too utopian a reform, we could imagine a basic income scheme that would allow some form of social contribution in the field of community economies (see Alexander 2015; Gough 2017).

Second, a decrease in overconsumption through reductions in hours in paid employment is a worthy sustainability solution that has not yet been addressed seriously in the global North (Schor 2005; 2010). Juliet Schor has acknowledged that in the present 'struggling' economies, the idea of reductions in working hours may be a hard sell since the conventional wisdom is that hard times should lead us to work longer and harder. However, the measures that result in higher hours in labour can be counterproductive by, for example, creating more demand only for a limited number of jobs. (Schor 2013, 6.) We believe that a radical redistribution of paid, alternatively paid and unpaid work can help tackle many welfare state problems simultaneously: overwork, unemployment, overconsumption and lack of meaning in work and everyday life. A recent study (Schiller et al. 2018), for example, found that a worktime reduction of 25% for full-time workers increased the time spent in recovery activities. This gave support to the conclusion that 'worktime reduction may be beneficial for long-term health and stress'– (ibid) and for cultivating community economies.

Finally, we see a broader conceptualisation of work as an important route to support community economies, sustainable lifestyles and welfare institutions in the midst of the sustainability transition.

4
Building upon, extending beyond: Small-scale food production within a Nordic welfare state

Pieta Hyvärinen

It goes without saying that small-scale food production in households and communities predates the formation of the welfare state. What is more intriguing is the persistence of these diverse livelihood practices through industrialisation and the establishment of centralised welfare systems. In contemporary Finland, alongside large-scale industrial agriculture, there is an undergrowth of food that is produced in backyard vegetable plots, allotment gardens and farming communities, or gathered from nature in the form of berries, mushrooms, fish and game. Small-scale food production within welfare states is even taking new forms, such as community-supported agriculture (European CSA Research Group 2016) and green care gardening (Rappe 2005), and is again practiced increasingly in urban environments (see Hagolani-Albov 2017) as well as in schools as part of educational curricula (Sipari 2013). The food system within Nordic welfare states is not, nor has ever been, a field populated only by industrial producers and individual consumers, but instead, it is characterised by diversity and multiplicity – and perhaps increasingly so, as environmental emergencies force a radical rethinking of how to provide for basic needs.

Despite its historical significance and current popularity, many forms and practices of small-scale food production are not acknowledged as economic activity through which livelihoods are sustained, especially in the context of a Nordic welfare state. Household food production is often seen rather as recreation (e. g. Natural Resources Institute Finland 2016a), or as domestic chores (e. g. Timonen 2005). The economic aspects of small-scale food production aimed at local markets have been studied more often from the point of view of rural entrepreneurship (e. g. Niemi and Pekkanen 2016) or consumer choice (e. g. Autio et al. 2013). Such interpretations can be seen as deriving from a capitalocentric economic discourse, in which non-capitalist economic forms and practices are understood primarily with reference to capitalism (Gibson-Graham 2006a, 6). Small-scale food production is thus seen as located within the feminine sphere of the household, complementary to capitalism, or in countries or areas 'peripheral' from the capitalist core, serving the consumerist markets with their products (see ibid., 6–7).

In this chapter, I focus on small-scale food production on a household level, but without making a sharp distinction between market-oriented and subsistence production. Rather, I understand small-scale food production as a spectrum of diverse economic practices within which the needs of producer/s are fulfilled and surplus if produced, being exchanged and invested in various ways, monetary as well as non-monetary. I explore small-scale food production as a landscape of economic difference rather than dominance, comprising of various interconnected capitalist and noncapitalist practices (see Gibson-Graham 2006b, 54; Harris

2009) and resisting the social construction of economy as singular and self-evident totality (see Mitchell 2007, 450–451).

For the purposes of examining the transformative potential of small-scale food production, I will use Ethan Miller's (2013) reading of community economies as refracted into three constituent elements: ontology, ethics and politics (see also Chapter 1). In the ontological moment, experimental ontology of radical economic difference, as described above, is combined with an anti-essentialist ontology of community by Jean-Luc Nancy (2000), in which community as *being-in-common* is understood as a condition of being itself, prior to all articulations of individual being (Miller 2013, 521). The ethical moment is described as an exposure of interdependencies for negotiation or contestation (ibid., 523). Ethical is therefore not understood as loaded with normative content, but rather as an open space for recognising and negotiating interdependencies (Gibson-Graham 2006b, x). Third element, the moment of politics, is that of collectively enacting 'positivity' with specific contents and outlines, grounded in place (Miller 2013, 525–526). Below I will further divide the moment of politics into three forms of economic possibility, inspired by feminist political imaginaries: politics of language, politics of the subject and politics of collective action (Gibson-Graham 2006b, xxxiii-xxxvii).

Based on the typology described above, I propose three interconnected perspectives to the transformative potential of small-scale food production within a Nordic welfare state for rearticulating and expanding the 'real utopia' of welfare states and the welfare ethos (see Chapter 1; Wright 2013) The arguments following are informed and inspired by ethnographic data collected in two case studies on community-based agriculture and urban beekeeping, conducted in southern Finland from 2015 to 2018. Firstly, I will discuss the scope of household food production and small-scale beekeeping in Finland, followed by a description of the entanglement of urban beekeeping and welfare state policies, in order to bring forth the radical heterogeneity and complex interconnections of sustenance practices within a welfare state. Secondly, I will examine the possibilities and tensions in widening the space for ethical economic negotiations already established within a welfare state towards non-human others through small-scale food production practices. Thirdly, I will explore small-scale food production as politics, possibly engendering new economic conceptualisations, subjectivities and bases for collective action. After examining these categories of transformative potential, I will conclude with critical remarks on some of the challenges posed by the possible increase of small-scale food production. The transformative potential of small-scale food production can be accompanied by serious pitfalls, and therefore its entanglements with the current and future manifestations of the Nordic welfare state should be scrutinised in detail to find out how to advance small-scale food production in a responsible manner.

Necessary transformation of food systems and welfare states
Before going into detail with small-scale food production, I will clarify two overlapping socio-ecological contexts: food systems and welfare states. I contextualise both from the perspective of necessary transformation, by which I refer to the ubiquity and indispensability of change. Neither food systems nor welfare states are stable entities but constantly in a state of flux, shifting from one regime to another (for changes in food systems, see Robinson 2004; for welfare states see Ellison 2005). Moreover, and in line with the diverse economies approach, enactments of both food systems and welfare states are always more complex than how they are portrayed in regime typologies, and they derive from a diversity of material, social, and cultural struggles and political imaginaries (cf. Gibson-Graham 2006b). The current manifestations of food systems and welfare states, often characterised by productivism and neoliberalisation respectively, should therefore not be seen as inevitable or 'natural' outcomes of any technological, social or

institutional development but rather as situated congealments of power relations and thus open to change through transformative politics (see Laclau and Mouffe 1985).

In the current era of widespread anthropogenic environmental turmoil, and especially given the pressing urgency of mitigating global warming, the need for transformations of food systems and welfare states is evident. Food production is a remarkable source of greenhouse gas emissions and other environmental damage (Norse 2003; Vermeulen et al. 2012), and it is in turn heavily affected by environmental changes and instabilities: for instance, climate change has various adverse effects on food production around the world (Hoegh-Guldberg et al. 2018). Particularly due to climate change, the number of undernourished people has been on the rise since 2014, reaching an estimated 821 million in 2017 (FAO et al. 2018). Additionally, malnutrition – lack of nutrients, proteins and vitamins due to poor food quality– is even more widespread, affecting over 2 billion people (Development Initiatives 2017). The productivist solution to the hunger problem is simply to increase production. Increasing production as business as usual, however, ignores the fact that calorie-wise, there is already enough food for all: along with hunger, the contemporary food system is also characterised by overproduction (see Chapter 5). Increasing the volume of food production alone will not solve the hunger problem, as problematic relations of production and unequal distribution of food are embedded in the very structure of the global food system (see Blay-Palmer 2010). Moreover, increase in food production without dramatically changing methods and techniques could on the contrary cause further instabilities in food security due to changing environmental conditions (see World Resources Institute 2018).

Nordic welfare states are closely connected to the abovementioned socio-environmental dilemmas of the global food system. Currently, Finland leans significantly on imported food products as well as production inputs such as agrochemicals and seeds (Knuuttila and

Vatanen 2015). Furthermore, all industrialised countries continue to consume planetary resources disproportionately, eroding the basis of present and future conditions needed for survival and wellbeing globally (see Dittrich et al. 2012). This unjust and unsustainable consumption is currently embedded in the very foundations of welfare state economies: welfare states, as we know them, are dependent on economic growth as measured by GDP (Bailey 2015; see also Chapter 1). Such extensive growth has been attested to not only as ultimately environmentally destructive, but also as long-term impossible given the finite resources of the earth. The promises of 'green growth' have repeatedly been debunked (e. g. Schandl et al. 2016; UNEP 2017), highlighting the necessity of decoupling the financial structures of welfare states from economic growth. The most recent IPCC report on climate change further underlines the urgency of halting the excessive use of fossil fuel derived energy and other resources, setting the limit of bearable global warming to 1.5°C (IPCC 2018). If that limit is exceeded, as will happen if current economic politics and policies are continued, welfare on a global scale, the least affected North included, will decline – especially given the accelerating pace of other forms of anthropogenic environmental destruction such as loss of biodiversity, degradation of fertile land and shortages of clean water.

A shift towards small-scale, low-input, agro-ecological and organic farming has been suggested as a viable way to tackle the complex socio-ecological issues around food production (McIntyre et al. 2009). Historically, small-scale food production has served as a base for most if not all civilizations before industrial agriculture, and still today small producers remain the backbone of food security at the global scale, producing 80% of the global food supply (FAO 2014). Given the efficiency of small-scale food production in terms of lower fossil energy and resource input (e. g. Markussen et al. 2014, Moore 2010), small-scale practices could help in limiting greenhouse gas emissions and even increasing carbon sequestration in soil (see Lal 2004). In addition to ecological benefits, small-scale farmers have also been recognised as the key players in combatting both hunger and poverty in the so-called Global South, not only contributing to household food security, but generating jobs and creating income for the wider community as well (FAO 2014). While challenges faced within welfare states are typically distinct from undernourishment and extreme poverty, increasing small-scale food production could have similarly far-reaching impacts. However, the hegemonic status occupied by productivism and growth-dependency as ways of enacting the food system and the welfare state prevents recognising, scrutinising, and realising the transformative potential of small-scale food production. Therefore, I will next focus on small-scale food producers as active participants in the rearticulation and restructuring of both food systems and welfare states.

Diverse practices of earthly survival

The significance and potential of small-scale food production within a Nordic welfare state can be illustrated by examples drawn from household food production and urban beekeeping in Finland. They offer a glimpse into the diversity of sustenance practices within welfare states, which, when scrutinised and contextualised as economic, could help to ontologically 'dis-order the capitalist economic landscape, to queer it and thereby dislocate capitalocentrism's hegemony' (Gibson-Graham 2006b, 77). Not only is food production within welfare states more diverse than often recognised, but practices of small-scale food production are also in many ways entangled with welfare state policies. The significance of non-salaried, feminised domestic and care work within welfare states has received attention (e. g. Hochschild 1989; Boje and Leira 2000), but the implications of small-scale food production for the functioning of welfare states is yet to be carefully studied.

Household food production is a common practice in Finland. In 2017, 29% of the adult population gardened edible plants (OSF 2018a), and in 2010, 58% of the population picked forest berries and 40% picked mushrooms for their own consumption (Finnish Forest Research Institute 2012). Non-commercial fishing is also popular, practiced by 40% of men and 20% of women (Natural Resources Institute Finland 2016b), and six percent of the population hold a hunting license (OSF 2018b). There are significant regional differences in household food production: for example, the average amount of forest berries picked by a household ranges from less than 10 litres in the southernmost regions to 40 litres in the North. 93% of all forest berries consumed by Finnish households are either self-picked or received as gifts or in barter. Household food production is, obviously, more prominent in rural than in urban households, as exemplified by potato production. In rural areas, households produce on average of almost half (46 kgs) of their annual consumption. In urban areas, the share of household production of consumed potatoes is seven kgs, around 11% of the annual consumption of 62 kgs. (Ylitalo 2008.)

If converted into market prices, the share of self-provisioned food items of household food consumption is relatively small, just over 2% in producer prices[15] (Ylitalo 2008). However, this does not necessarily implicate an insignificance of household food production for individual households from a sustenance perspective, not to mention other motivations and meanings of producing one's own food. In a study conducted among household food producers in Finland, more affordable food was stated to be a significant motivation factor by around 40% of the respondents (Koivusilta et al. 2018, 28). In another, European-

---

15   The data is not available in consumer prices, in which the percentage would be significantly higher: for example, the producer price for potato is less than €0.20/kg (OSF 2018c), whereas the consumer price is around €0.90/kg (OSF 2018d).

wide survey, around 5% of Western European households reported producing over 50% of their food consumption (Alber and Kohler 2008, 117). Household food production can indeed be understood as contributing to household food security within welfare states as well, even if not in such a drastic sense as is often the case in the absence of institutional welfare systems (see FAO 2014). This is further underlined by the fact that the affordability of food was more significant a motivator for people with a lower socio-economic status and hence, presumably, lower income (Koivusilta et al 2018, 31).

However, as highlighted by Jehlicka et al. in the context of post-soviet Czechia (2013), household food production is more than a coping strategy for the poor. There is a variety of motivations for household food production in Finland as well, ranging from access to more healthy food, meaningful use of time, to environmental and animal welfare concerns (Koivusilta et al. 2018, 27–30). Therefore, household food production can be seen as not only complementary to welfare state food security measures, but also as an active contribution to human and non-human wellbeing (ibid., 12–13). In addition to experiencing *more* wellbeing, wellbeing experienced in or pursued by small-scale food production might differ qualitatively from wellbeing measured in GDP. This diversification of the understandings of wellbeing can be understood as a necessary step in transforming welfare systems in accordance with the radical reductions in production and consumption of energy and use of natural resources (see also Hirvilammi and Helne 2014; Smith 2018).

In addition to berries and potatoes, some special food products are extensively produced by small-scale producers: it is estimated that two thirds of Finnish honey is produced by amateur or part-time beekeepers with less than 100 colonies (E.-L. Korpela, personal communication, October 2, 2018). Even though small producers often sell at least part of their honey on the market, small-scale beekeeping is not organised solely according to the logic of profit making, and therefore it can also be seen as disrupting the capitalocentric understanding of food systems. In my ethnographic study, high honey yields and sales were among a variety of motivations for beekeeping, including pollination of garden plants, social relations, interest in nature, sustaining mental vigour and increasing overall wellbeing. Unprofitability of small-scale beekeeping in conventional economic terms was widely recognised: earnings from honey typically cover production costs – equipment, feeding, packaging, new queens – but compensation for work is not usually counted in at all, or only partially. Measured in conventional economic terms, the wage in professional beekeeping can be as low as 6.50 euros per hour (Natural Resources Institute Finland 2015), and as small-scale beekeeping practices are typically even more time-consuming, the hourly income, if calculated, would be even lower.

Given the significance of honeybees as pollinators (Kleijn et al. 2015), it is safe to assume that small-scale beekeeping contributes remarkably to both industrial and informal food production in Finland. Therefore, it can be argued, that the most fundamental material base of welfare states is partly sustained by informal work in beekeeping, in a similar way as institutional social protection is complemented and supported by household food production as described above. This is, however, only one aspect in the complex relationship between welfare states and small-scale food production practices. Welfare policies and services in turn enable and even support small scale food production. For instance, beekeepers' high average age of 57 (FBA 2015), means many of them enjoy old age pensions, and also the need for (public) health care services increases in old age. Additionally, especially in urban beekeeping, the material infrastructure provided and maintained by the still relatively well-funded public sector plays a significant role, at times even directly supporting beekeepers by allowing the use of wastelands for apiaries and even premises such as sheds for storage. Furthermore, the high level of trust and stability in welfare states might allow beekeepers to operate without being excessively concerned with urban beehives being harassed or stolen. In this way, small-scale food production can be both seen as filling the social and ecological gaps that public services leave and harnessing the surplus of welfare states (see Chapter 1).

However, welfare state policies can also cause tensions in small-scale food production. The pressure to participate in the formal labour markets is increasing as welfare is being transformed with the activation paradigm (see Chapter 3), and time available for food production can become scarce. This can lead to difficult choices in time-consuming and laborious practices such as beekeeping. In my research data, one former beekeeper couple had chosen to invite other beekeepers to take over their home yard apiary, as they preferred to have bees nearby despite giving up beekeeping due to lack of time. Another urban beekeeper ceased keeping bees after a few hard and honey-poor years when time-limited due to starting her own business. Several have reduced the number of colonies due to lack of time, but also due to preferring close engagement with the bees and honey over production-centred practices.

Small-scale food production vividly illustrates the opening of yet unthought possibilities of communities and economies. Coexisting (peacefully or not) with the sustenance policies of the welfare state, there are diverse practices of 'earthly survival' (see Haraway 2016) which are viable, life-sustaining and purposefully pursued. Embodied in the entanglements of welfare state policies and small-scale food production practices there are also various ways on economic *being-in-common* based on interdependencies, whether recognised and acted upon or not (Gibson-Graham 2006b, 84, 88). Next, I proceed to examine negotiations over some of the most essential interdependencies in food production.

Negotiating multispecies interdependencies
Nordic welfare states are characterised by a high level of universalism, within which people are attributed rights by virtue of

membership in a particular community (Kildal and Kuhnle 2005). Given that these rights address questions of survival and wellbeing in particular, the welfare state can be understood as a sort of an institutionalised communal space akin to community economies 'in which individual and collective subjects negotiate questions of livelihood and interdependence and (re)consruct themselves in the process' (Gibson-Graham 2006b, x; see also Chapter 1). Even though these negotiations often take place far from the individual subjects and their livelihoods, they are usually located within democratic structures and institutions, which at least in principle enable citizen participation. However, the recognition of socio-ecological interdependencies is severely limited, as shown by the continuing contribution of welfare states to global environmental destruction (see Hirvilammi and Helne 2014). Production and consumption of food and other commodities in welfare states affect livelihoods beyond national borders and species boundaries, but the economic negotiations within welfare state universalism do not, by definition, consider the needs of other than a particular group of people.

Practices of small-scale food production enable recognising and negotiating interdependencies in ways which might extend beyond the current limitations of welfare state universalism at least in terms of interspecies relations. I will next focus on the possibilities of small-scale food production to challenge the ways in which non-human nature is positioned as the inferior counterpart in a hierarchical dualism as is symptomatic to the Western philosophical tradition (e.g. Plumwood 1993). I argue that situated knowledge production and affective engagements constitute the key elements in enacting interspecies relations differently within small-scale food production, opening up ethical space for negotiating interdependencies, which are rendered invisible in industrial food production and capitalist food markets. To ground my arguments, I will first introduce the companion species approach by Donna Haraway (2008), which helps to

4 – Small-scale food production

conceptualise the extension of the ethical moment of community economies construction towards the non-human world.

The companion species approach means understanding humans as always already entangled with the non-human nature in mutually constitutive networks. Haraway questions the individuality of a human (or a member of any species), as well as dualist categorisations such as nature/culture and human/animal. According to Haraway, '[t]o be one is always to *become with* many' (2008, 4, emphasis in the original). For Haraway, non-human others are active participants in the making of culture and society, and, one could add, economy in companion species networks. In these networks 'being' is continuous *becoming with*, and is devoid of any predefined purpose (Haraway 2008). This notion bears resemblance to the understanding of community as *being-in-common* in the community economies approach (see Gibson-Graham 2006b, Nancy 2000).

Food and its production exemplify the mutual constitutiveness of companion species networks: food *is* non-human others, made edible by cultivating, selective breeding and preparation in complex multispecies constellations. However, these networks are often not visible in the contemporary food systems (see e.g. Franklin 1999; Tsing 2015). Capitalist production and markets tend to efface the specificities of any relations and connections beyond the immediate transactions (Gibson-Graham 2006b, 83; see also Callon 1998; Polanyi 2001, original 1944), concealing the companion species networks in which eating takes place. The ethical tensions in food production are not only based on the inevitable consumption of other species for bodily reproduction, but are rather political in nature, deriving from different material, cultural and social arrangements of food systems. Therefore, recognising and acting upon the 'differential relationalities' of eating is essential 'if response and regard are to have any meaning personally and politically' (Haraway 2008, 295).

Small-scale food production includes and encourages

interspecies relations that are distinct from the commodified and market-mediated relations enacted in industrial food systems. Koivusilta et al. (2018, 39–40) highlight this from the point of view of domestic animals: improving animal welfare is a significant motivation for keeping animals for food production. Accordingly, in small-scale beekeeping courses, participants are guided to recognise multispecies interdependencies – or, following Haraway, companion species networks – and to engage responsively with non-human others, in addition to humans: primarily with the bees but also with other animals and even inanimate objects such as bee products and hive materials.

Reformulating interspecies relations in small-scale food production is not necessarily limited to domestic animals. In a case study on community-based agriculture, I analysed manual weeding practices as situated multispecies knowledge production, in which the needs of non-human others are intertwined within communal decision-making on future agricultural measures (Hyvärinen 2017; see also Roelvink 2015). Manual weed management is typical in small-scale gardening and agriculture, organised often as alternatively paid or unpaid work, but rarely practiced in industrial farming in welfare states due to high labour expenses. In the farming communities the slow, bodily practices of weeding appeared as a constant, multisensory observation in which the various non-human others of the field became noticed: one could not ignore how the different plants were growing, and what was the condition of the living soil. Observations were shared with other field workers during breaks or after work and combined with experiences and existing knowledge or even information looked up on the internet. This kind of situated knowledge production (Haraway 1988) responds to the particular questions at hand instead of aiming at universality, and it also recognises the 'object' of inquiry – here the agricultural ecosystem – as an active part of the process. In the process of situated knowledge production, companion species networks are knit

4 – Small-scale food production

more closely together, in relation to the communities' livelihoods: In the farming communities, situated knowledge produced through weeding guided short- as well as long-term farming practices, which aimed at providing for survival and wellbeing for the community. Weeding made companion species networks of food production visible and part of negotiations over livelihoods, widening the scope of ethical economic negotiations towards non-human others (Hyvärinen 2017; see also Gibson-Graham 2006b, 81).

Another aspect in reformulating the space for ethical negotiations in small-scale food production are the affective engagements formed in everyday food production practices. Beekeeping serves as a case in point with its intimate but troubled relationship between humans and bees. Affective engagement in urban beekeeping is eloquently described by Mary Moore and Lisa Jean Kosut (2013):

> 'Beekeepers feel a buzz, a slight intoxication, enthusiasm, and exhilaration in the presence of these insects. This feeling is what we term the affective buzz, a transformation through bonding with the bees. [--] Like some form of insect drug, bees have physiological effect on the body, affecting the way we think, act, and move.' (Moore and Kosut 2013, 56–57)

The affective buzz that the authors describe can also be noticed in an explicit manifestation of *becoming with* in companion species networks: the urban beekeepers' altered perception or experience of their surroundings. Even when the bees are not present, beekeepers may perceive the weather and the plants from the perspective of the bees: how the flowers are blooming, what is the weather like for the bees to fly or, during the winter, to survive – as if they could share the lifeworld of a bee colony (see also Maderson and Wynne-Jones 2016, 93).

Interestingly, affective engagements in beekeeping are not

based on the experienced sameness or relatability. Rather, it is the overwhelming otherness of these insects that seems to be a central factor in the fascination and joy that humans experience in their proximity (see also Moore and Kosut 2013, 55). Hugh Raffles (2011, 44) describes insect-human relations as 'a deep, dead space without reciprocity, recognition or redemption.' Bees, like any insects, are ultimately unintelligible from the human perspective, but the human-bee cooperation in beekeeping, however ambiguous, seems to bridge this deep (in)difference enough to display bees' otherness as something to embrace rather than something to turn away from. This can be understood as a transformative act from the perspective of ethical economic negotiations, extending their scope far beyond welfare state universalism that is based on shared citizenship or residency – and, first of all, on membership of the human species.

Unlearning the commodification of non-humans and respectively learning to be affected by these 'earth others' (Roelvink 2015) is an onto-epistemologically crucial process in building more liveable futures (see Haraway 2016). Small-scale food production has the potential to alter the relations between humans and non-human others by pointing out vital interdependencies in the processes of situated knowledge production and by enabling practices in which humans are literally affectively touched by other species (see also Puig de la Bellacasa 2017). The processes of becoming *with* take tangible forms in small-scale food production through weeds, bees and multiple others with whom the necessities of life and diverse forms of wellbeing are produced.

Nevertheless, from an ethical perspective small-scale food production is not devoid of problems: in Haraway's words, 'there is no way to eat and not to kill' (2008, 295), as the interspecies relations in food production are more often *indigestive* than symbiotic (ibid., 287, 300). Sentient beings are slaughtered and consumed in animal production regardless of its scale. Also beekeeping and even vegetable production have adverse or contradictory effects on non-human others, however considerately practiced. Nevertheless, as mentioned, the ethical moment in constructing community economies does not imply any universal, definitive answers to how or with what normative content the negotiations over interdependencies are to be accomplished (Miller 2013, 523). The radical critique towards capitalism lies in the situated and particular recognition and the acting upon interdependencies in contrast to obscuring or denying them (Miller 2013; Gibson-Graham 2006b, 84). In small-scale food production the non-human others are not concealed in long chains of market transactions, but rather relating with them acts as a starting point to re-imagine and remake future practices of survival and wellbeing (cf. Gibson-Graham 2006b, 98, 194). Recognising non-human agencies, consciousness, and even personalities, and simultaneously acknowledging the inescapable necessity of consuming other species, makes small-scale food production a praxis of 'staying with the trouble' (Haraway 2016), thereby keeping the ethical space open to constant negotiations over multispecies interdependencies.

Counterhegemonies in action
The politics of possibility in community economies framework leans on the feminist movement, more precisely 'the complex intermixing of alternative discourses, shared language, embodied practices, self-cultivation, emplaced actions, and global transformation associated with second-wave feminism' (Gibson-Graham 2006b, xxiv). The transformative power of feminism is ubiquitous and uncoordinated but at the same time firmly grounded in subjectivities and places, which are, however, always unfixed and incomplete: sites of becoming and openings for politics (ibid., xxxiii). Politics of economic possibility operates on the grounds of these open 'negativities', aiming at creating novel economic 'positivities' through the politics of language, politics of the subject, and collective action (ibid., xxxiv–xxxvii; Miller 2013, 525–526). Traces of all three can be located in the field of

small-scale food production, possibly offering alternatives to the hegemonic arrangements of food systems and welfare states.

First, dislodging capitalocentric conceptualisations and diversifying the understandings of economic practices and relations could contribute to widening the discursive space in which other economies become possible. Small-scale food production is based on such economic practices which hardly fit the narrow capitalocentric conceptualisations of the economy (Gibson-Graham 2006a; Cameron and Gordon 2010). Work in small-scale food production is not organised only as wage labour, but also as various forms of alternatively paid or non-paid labour (Hyvärinen 2017; see Gibson-Graham 2006b, 71). Sometimes the practices are not even considered as work by the small producers themselves, despite being burdensome and time-consuming. This reflects the common understanding of work as including wage labour only. Often, however, urban beekeepers and members of the farming communities reach far beyond conventional capitalocentric views in their deliberations: work is considered as a community-building activity, as mental and spiritual as well as physical activity, and as activity performed by non-humans as well as by humans (see also Chapter 3).

Accordingly, practices and relations of exchange appear as diverse in small-scale food production. Even though market relations exist within the small-scale food production sector, operations in the sector are not primarily defined by competitiveness as is the case of mainstream market economy. Rather, diverse forms of value are at play when defining the terms of exchange, often based on interaction between people (see Chapter 2) or even species. This is illustrated, for example, by the complex and often contested process of defining a suitable price for home produced honey in urban beekeeping. In my data, the price was not only defined by the production costs, whether or not it included compensation for labour, but it was also affected by the regular customers' willingness or ability to pay. In addition, other beekeepers' subsistence needs were taken into account by avoiding dumping prices, and sometimes even the hard work done by the bees was recognised as valuable. Moreover, small-scale food production can be considered as questioning the preferability of mainstream (food) markets: household food producers are motivated by the access to pure and healthy food, the origins of which they know (Koivusilta et al. 2018, 28), implying a perceived untrustworthiness of the mainstream food markets and possibly opening up space for alternatives (see also Forssell 2017).

For Gibson-Graham (2006b, xxxvi), politics of the subject include 'mobilization and transformation of desires, cultivation of capacities, and the making of new identifications' – constructing of new economic subjects which relate to each other in interdependent ways (ibid., 81). Small-scale food production offers subject positions and identifications which deviate from those based on wage labour, and competitive markets relations (see Trauger and Passidomo 2012). The study by Koivusilta et al. (2018, 27–30) suggests that household food production could enable identification with a variety of positive characteristics, such as meaningfulness, skillfulness, eagerness to learn, close connection to nature in general and domestic animals in particular, environmental responsibility and a healthy lifestyle. Small-scale food production practices can be a source of joy and pride, often manifested through food products, as attested by, for example, beekeepers' descriptions of their own home-produced honey.

Due to its potentiality in modifying social identities and self-perception in a positive way, small-scale food production and especially gardening has been used in mental health, elderly and disabled care historically and increasingly also today, nowadays termed as 'green care' (see Rappe 2005; Sempik et al. 2010). From the perspective of subject formation, the concept can be understood as carrying a double meaning: who or what is caring for and whom or what is taken care of? Positioning oneself as caring for other beings by cultivating and maintaining them or, when it comes to human others, by feeding them with self-produced food can enable re-evaluation of self-centered subject positions (see Puig de la Bellacasa 2017). In relation to the increasingly precarious working life, small-scale food production can also help in distancing oneself from unreachable career pursuits and work ethics driven by consumerism and redirect competence building (see Chapter 3). There is expertise to be gained and identities to be constructed in a variety of food production areas, as exemplified by the urban beekeepers and vegetable farmers, but also by mushroom foragers, fishers, orchardists, brewers, fermenters, and so on.

In such a diverse field of food production activities and actors, there is no singular collective to be formed as a base for collective action. Collectives are always situated and grounded in a particular place and time – but, significantly, potentially in *any* context (Gibson-Graham 2006b, xxxvii–xxxviii). The place-bound small-scale food production can therefore serve as a ground for collective action especially in relation to political struggles over a specific geographical area, as for example analysed in urban settings by Koopmans et al. (2017) as processes of place-making. However, the political aims of food-production-based collective organising are not necessarily limited to the specificities of a particular place, as exemplified by the above mentioned farming communities which aimed to achieve ecological sustainability and social justice through non-conventional, collective farming practices. Small-scale food producers can also form political collectives together with larger-scale producers, like urban beekeepers taking part in the Finnish Beekeepers' Association or farming communities participating in the Finnish Organic Association which brings together organic farmers of all scales of operation.

Politics of collective action can be examined not only in their present form, but tentatively as possible means of increasing small-scale food production within a welfare state. Hindrances for increasing household food production include experienced lack of

4 – Small-scale food production

time and storage space, but also lack of land, money, possibilities for animal husbandry and knowledge (Koivusilta et al. 2018, 35). Collective action, aiming at transforming specific welfare state policies or targeted at particular institutions could be used to overcome such deficiencies. Lack of time could be resolved by restricting working hours in wage labour by legislation, of which there are numerous examples in the history of welfare states. Lack of storage and arable land could be tackled by designating more space for agricultural activities and products by creating new building regulations and by using already existing spatial planning measures. Public social investments could be used for financing the development of communal food production facilities, and the existing educational infrastructure in turn for increasing knowledge on food production techniques and skills, in addition to the already existing knowledge commons in public libraries and available through universal internet access. If small-scale food production would be politicised through conscious collective action efforts, the existing welfare state institutions could be harnessed to promote and facilitate these practices, turning them from the state of inaction to purposefully creating favourable conditions for small-scale food production or even directly assisting its expansion (see Chapter 1).

Conclusions
Instead of a peripheral or anachronistic activity, as suggested by a capitalocentric understanding of the economic, small-scale food production is a widespread and manifold phenomenon with capacities to transform future food systems and welfare. However, there are no guarantees of how an increase in small-scale food production would change societies or even the environmental impact of food production. There are fossil fuel-powered or otherwise environmentally detrimental practices in small-scale food production as well, as many of them have been formed during the era of cheap fossil energy and require transformation

to fit into the post-fossil future. However, many practices predate the abundance of affordable fossil fuels or have more recently been intentionally shaped to avoid excessive use of energy and other resources. In industrial agriculture a shift from fossil fuel dependency to less energy intensive production methods and renewable resources can be considerably more challenging (see Günther 2001).

Socially and politically as well, small-scale food production enables multiple readings, of which I have above focused on the ones that build upon and extend beyond welfare state policies. However, increase in small-scale food production can also be construed as fundamentally incompatible with financing welfare services: increasing self-sufficiency could result in reduced revenues from income and value-added taxation. Moreover, it could be used as a justification for growing individual and gendered[16] responsibilities of basic survival needs and further cuts on social benefits, exacerbating social inequalities. In accordance with neoliberal austerity it is easy to imagine a moralising public discussion about the 'lazy grasshoppers' who failed to gather enough provisions for the winter and have to be then fed from the common pool. Increasing importance of small-scale food production has also the potential for fuelling nationalist tendencies built upon a mythical, naturalised connection between a homogenous population and the natural resources in a particular area, protected by strict border control.

When pursuing an equitable post-growth future, increasing small-scale food production should not be understood as a replacement of welfare services and policies as a sort of a 'commons fix' (see Chapter 1). Physically arduous labour is not feasible for all

---

16   As small-scale food production includes everyday household work practices which have traditionally been strictly gender segregated (or at least depicted as such) in the Nordic societies (see Peltonen 1999), it is possible that such segregation continues and is strengthened despite currently successful gender equality policies within the Nordic welfare states.

and also access to land and other resources, knowledge and time are all unevenly distributed. Should small-scale food production increase, welfare state-like policies would still be needed to ensure equal access to food regardless of one's individual capacities and resources. Comprehensive welfare would also help to maintain social stability and mutual trust in a situation where in the absence of widely available fossil energy the fundamental precariousness of life – human vulnerability to the unstable processes of air, land and water – is revealed (see Tsing 2015). From the diverse economies perspective, small-scale food production, even with a significant increase in volume, would be only one of many forms and aspects of the future food and welfare systems.

Welfare states as institutional and political enactments of a particular ethos of universality and equality can serve as a platform for increasing small-scale food production without overemphasising individual responsibility. Despite the challenges the welfare ethos and ideal are currently encountering, ideologically the platform is still relatively well-founded, as collectively financed welfare policies continue to enjoy high public support (Svallfors 2012, 5–6). Strengthening and expanding this solidarity, currently enacted within national and species boundaries, is a process in which the transformative ontological, ethical and political potential of community economies can prove useful, as illustrated above in terms of food production.

The increase in the scope or significance of small-scale food production does not involve any inevitable outcomes. Therefore, no scenario described above should be deemed as adequate grounds to refrain from nor to uncritically embrace small-scale food production as present and future livelihood practice. Outlining different prospects and possibilities aims at highlighting the political character of such transitions and reminding us of the need for ethical consideration in relation to them. Transforming welfare states does not happen only by increasing small-scale food production, but on many fronts simultaneously. Together with, for instance, social welfare innovations like universal basic income or new forms of markets often termed as the 'sharing economy', small-scale food production might contribute to sustaining and developing welfare responsively.

Given the persistent hegemonies of productivism and growth-dependency, radical institutional and ideological reforms in food systems and welfare states might seem unlikely or even impossible to achieve. However, compared with the massive challenges in developing or even sustaining food security and welfare services in the long run if the 1.5 °C target in global warming is exceeded, the challenges related to restructuring the economic politics, practices and discourses of food and welfare systems are, after all, manageable. Examining small-scale food production as construction of community economies could enable engaging academically as well as politically with such an extensive and unpredictable, but also situated transformation – enacting food politics of becoming in place (see Gibson-Graham 2006b, xxiv).

5
Commoning surplus food in Finland – actors and tensions

Anna-Maria Isola and Janne Laiho

Unsalable food has considerable market value, yet it is possessed by no-one. It is a resource that basically no one owns, but which factually exists. In this chapter, we examine surplus food as a commons, a decommodified good. Surplus food attracts various regulative actors and functions. It is a social node that gathers institutions, activists and lay people together.

Surplus food does not create a permanent community economy in the sense that Gibson-Graham (2008) understands it. However, it creates economic activity in the overlap of market economy, social security and self-sufficiency. It may for instance supplement inadequate income, improve purchasing power or make it possible for one to not participate in the market economy. Surplus food is shared in foodbanks where people create temporary community economies. Surplus also may create new small-scale community economies, such as community fridges.

There is a variety of ontological premises associated with surplus food of which one gets clues by looking at related terms. One talks about food aid, another refers to food waste and leftovers, while yet others emphasize the problem of overproduction typical of the market economy and climatic effects associated with it. What abovementioned different contexts have in common is that they are different modulations of the phenomenon, in which unsalable yet edible food is recognised as a resource. While surplus food is a positive commons, resource, it is also an environmental problem, this is, a commons in a negative sense. Due to the climate issue, the impetus to control surplus belongs to all: locally, regionally, nationally and globally.

Three different interests and tensions are examined in this chapter. Firstly, food surplus is an environmental problem. Secondly, surplus food is currently governed by sharing it with poor people. Thirdly, sharing surplus to poor people through foodbanks does alleviate poverty, but it is puzzling in terms of universal rights and sufficient minimum income supposedly provided by the welfare state.

Food surplus as a commons organizes social life locally, particularly in local foodbanks, but in the long run it also may re-organize the principles of the welfare state. The multilateral connections and collaboration between the actors – local communities, retailers, charity organisations, public sector actors and food surplus activists – are viewed as social nodes. This chapter is based on the extended case study method to explore both the repertoire of the meanings and processes of negotiations concerning food surplus (see Burawoy 1989, 3, 16–24). The data gathering included ethnography at a food surplus terminal, nine excursions to food surplus distribution points, eight interviews, and surplus food related documents. It involved also taking part in two communal dinners, visiting a waste food restaurant, a food waste shop, and a non-profit open 'community fridge'.

The most common contexts of food surplus

It was understood already several decades ago that persistent overproduction can be regarded as a failure of agricultural policy (European Community 1986; Buttel 2003; FAO 2011) and the market economy. Producers of goods and services will keep producing and supplying the market as long as the marginal profits from production are higher than is an alternative course of action. The globalized agro-food system maintains unsustainable overproduction, but the problem of surplus could however be solved, little by little, through supporting and making consumer choices favouring small scale or local co-operatives, or community economies in general.

However, commercial capital creates downward price pressures on farmers who work within the state–capital nexus that institutionalizes overproduction (Snyder 2015). Commercial capital then destroys the seeds of other kind of systems by putting more competitive pressure on small-scale producers and alternative food systems. There are fundamental incompatibilities between the food regime governed by the logic of commercial capital and alternative systems, democratically designed to develop sustainable food culture and human capacities (see Chapters 3–4; Nousiainen et al. 2009).

Producers might not always be able to meet demand. However, as potential profit exists in such a case, it is likely that supply and/or market prices will increase until a new equilibrium is reached. In the case of insufficient supply, the only change required to reach equilibrium is a change in output and/or prices, with no action to be taken with regards to inventory already produced. In contrast, in the case of excess production, there is no mechanism to cancel production that has already taken place. Producers of goods will need to resort to measures such as price differentiation in order to get rid of excess production.

Overproduction is more likely than underproduction, as long as the expected cost of the former does not exceed the expected profit loss associated with the latter, *ceteris paribus*. In the Western world and in the case of foodstuffs, this seems to be the typical case: it is very rare that a given food product is not available on a given day at a grocery store due to insufficient supply.

If the surplus food is not drawn back into the market or distributed as food aid, it becomes waste. Food waste is recognized as a growing environmental problem all over the First World. In Finland, 23 kilograms of food per person is being disposed of annually. The monetary value of household food waste has been illustrated by comparing it with a spa vacation for the whole family and with eight annual visits to a movie theatre. The combined food waste of households, industry, trade and restaurant services amounts to approximately 335-460 million kilograms annually, with a value of 500 million euro. The climate impact of the entire life cycle of materials and products have in turn been compared with the combined carbon dioxide emissions of 100 000 average cars. (Silvennoinen et. al 2013)

Bradshaw (2018, 12, 327–330; see also Evans and Nagele 2018) states that categorizing food as waste is a consequence of political and value-laden practices, which completely neglect the aim of preventing foodstuff from becoming waste. In 2013, the Finnish Food Safety Authority (Evira) introduced guidelines on how to utilise 'food waste' and prevent it from getting into landfill. According to the guidelines, primary producers, breeders, storages, wholesalers, grocery stores, mass caterers and restaurants are allowed to deliver unsalable but edible food to consumers, either directly or through charity organisations. (Evira 2017.) Re-commodification of surplus food is allowed to take place through grocery stores specializing in food waste, waste food restaurants, and other commercial operators within a circular economy. Private households are not officially allowed to redistribute their leftovers. In addition to official actors, climate activists operate in the area of food waste by raising discussions on how much carbon dioxide is emitted as a result of surplus food that ends up as food waste.

Surplus food has been abundantly examined from the point of view of food aid thus far. Food aid is a common way to distribute surplus food through foodbanks to those of little income. Foodbanks have existed in Finland for several decades, but they became a permanent phenomenon during the depression of the 1990's, when the level of social security was also lowered (Kuivalainen and Nelson 2013). During that same period, food aid become an established phenomenon across the first world. (Silvasti and Karjalainen 2014, 73–76; de Armiño 2014; Dowler 2014; Silvasti 2015, 474.) Foodbanks have been left to grow with little attention before they recently re-emerged in public discourse.

Whereas a few decades ago, foodbanks were mostly frequented by the homeless and substance abusers, the clientele has since become more diverse in its composition. They have brought people of low income, pensioners, low-income families with children and single mothers out onto the streets, into public view. (Laihiala 2018, 5–6.) It is known that the economic vulnerability of those standing in breadlines is manifested as difficulties in dealing with debt and well as not being able to make ends meet. Multifaceted disadvantage has also accumulated among them: every third person experienced resorting to food aid as shameful, women considered it more socially stigmatizing than men did. Lining-up is a social activity, foodbanks are a place for giving and receiving peer support. (Ohisalo et al. 2015, 443; Salonen et al. 2018; Laihiala 2018.)

Food aid appears to be a more integrally institutionalized part of the Finnish society. This has to do with the fact that in the Nordic welfare state on one hand the goal of decommodification has a less important role, and on the other hand, individual responsibility has been given more emphasis (see Chapter 1). Current plans for organizing food aid institutionally include merging the Fund for European Aid to the Most Deprived, the EU Programme for Employment and Social Innovation, the EU Health Programme, and the European Social Fund (European Social Fund Plus 2018; Chambon 2011). It is notable that the new European Social Fund Plus focuses on food aid in particular and does not promote a higher basic economic security. These plans have affected Finnish social policy too, as Finnish authorities had to take a stance on public food aid. In December 2017, The Ministry of Social Affairs and Health issued a bulletin taking an indirect stance towards EU plans. In the bulletin, food aid was discussed as a part of civil society, therefore not part of the Finnish social security system.

> 'Instead of handing out food aid, it is important to reach for overall and long-term improvement and support for people's everyday life. This can be accomplished through good social policy, the legislation of which falls under the responsibility of the Ministry. In everyday work, social services meeting with the needs of the customers, and organizational work that supports the work of civil servants, are in a key position.' (MoSAaH 2017, translation by the authors).

The distribution of surplus as food aid threatens the foundations of the welfare state, at least to some extent. Charitable food is not an answer to hunger, while a decent minimum income is (Silvasti and Riches 2014, 192; Silvasti 2015, 476). However, the redistribution of surplus food through charity organizations has become an institutionalised practice that reproduces income inequality and legitimizes personal generosity as the response to a structural problem (Poppendieck 1999; Silvasti and Riches 2014, 207–208). The growth of kindness and injustice, and charity and poverty, are intertwined. Based on a large ethnographic research, Janet Poppendieck (1999, 5) found that flourishing charity is both a symptom and a cause of society's failure to deal with increasing inequality and income poverty. Charity indeed treats the wounds of inequality, but simultaneously it also relieves pressure from redressing income inequality on a large scale. As a consequence, more fundamental social policy measurements can be brushed aside when foodbanks are called out to for help. Food aid even de-politicizes hunger and draws media attention away from governmental welfare schemes. (Poppendieck 1999; Silvasti and Riches 2014.)

Charity organisations benefit from institutionalized food charity (Silvasti and Riches, 2014 , 196–197). Religious or charity organisations are able to take roles as middlemen in making surplus production more acceptable and transforming it into a virtue (Salonen 2016; 2017). Also retailers benefit, as their waste disposal costs are lowered, and they appear to take more responsibility in society (see Silvasti and Riches 2014, 195–196; Calvo-Porral et al. 2016). Food aid thus offers a platform for charity work and for building a brand that benefits corporations and charity organizations. A harmful side effect is that the institutionalized distribution of food waste produces mechanisms through which the role of welfare states in guaranteeing a decent life to their citizens, based on the principle of universalism, is hindered (see Bradshaw 2018; Silvasti and Riches 2014).

As noted in Chapter 1, in the Nordic welfare states, power has been transferred from local associations and governments to central governments. Its financial and material linkage with capitalist economy is so strong that the centralized power might be in risk of being occupied by big corporations. From this point of view, surplus food is interesting: on one hand, sharing it through foodbanks promotes the gradual move into principles of residual distribution of well-being, as opposed to universalism that has long been emphasized by the welfare state. On the other hand, surplus as a commons may generate the effect of returning power from the state and corporations to local economies, where the rules over a commons can be negotiated independently of the market and the state.

Commons as a method of organisation

A commons is a pool of material or immaterial resources that are managed by communities or groups for collective and individual purposes. Material commons, such as drinking water, air, seeds, minerals, the ozone layer, and forests, often go over- or misused. Other kinds of common resources such as creative resources, common knowledge, social values and rules, emerge as commons through communication (Nelson 2016, 3–4).

Capitalism, the market economy, the welfare state, and a commons, are all social systems of organisation. A commons is formed from and organized through resources that are not simply economic. These resources need to be activated through *commoning:* social practices used by commoners (De Angelis 2007; 2013; Nelson 2016). In this kind of social system, not only resources are shared and managed in everyday practices, but also communities and life itself are reproduced in non-commodified ways.

Managing a resource as a commons decentralizes power and invites people's participation. Commoning incorporates open-ended value-negotiating processes. The commons and commoning are means for democratic processes to function, from negotiating freedoms and responsibilities to influencing modes of (re)production (Nelson 2016, 6; De Angelis 2013, 606; Linebaugh 2008). The democratic power of the commons is rooted in routines and daily practices that are tied to culture and history.

Commoning allows deliberative democracy to develop, specifically due to face-to face communication. However, as with any social system, commoning is a system of exclusion. Constructing a commons implies creating rules on participation and exclusion from it (Nelson 2016, 7). Likewise, different actors want to attach community-originated rules to food surplus on who is entitled to it, and whether it will be distributed for no charge, or perhaps in exchange for labour.

Commons might also be needed and utilised by capitalism. From the point of view of capital, the need for a 'commons fix' (see Introduction) is twofold. On the one hand, capital needs new strategies to maintain growth and accumulation. And on the other, capital needs a commons to fix the devastation it creates for social relations and the environment. It follows that a commons may be integrated into capital or it may reconstruct new social terrain. By the same token, a commons may result in either emancipation or oppression.

Massimo De Angelis (2013) notes that a commons is a social force that is able to create systems independent from capital, alternative ways of social production, and it could even entail solutions to social and ecological injustice. No one knows in advance the outcome of the process of commons being born and them becoming governed, as it depends on the fluid process of a commons democracy.

Civil society and the welfare state as a new social node in the field of food surplus

The 1980s saw the emergence of new actors in the field of food surplus, while earlier it was only charities and retailers working together. These new actors demanded changes to food aid practices. The church social work organisations in one large Finnish city decided that breadlines must be gotten rid of: not because of a will to end food aid, but because queueing outside was seen as humiliating. Gradually the civil society groups, city government and church organisation within this city took it as a common objective. Changing established practices was heavy work, and it was not before the 2000s when these actors were able to take decisive steps from talk to action.

> 'Our starting point has been that we want to get rid of breadlines entirely. And it is just terribly slow work, it sure isn't something which happens in a moment, it demands networking skills and discussion, and we have very small teams and no levers for controlling the activities of associations that distribute food aid.' (A church social worker)

In addition to handing out the usual food bags, these organisations began offering donated food in the form of communal meals. Retailers, NGOs and city representatives got together to decide on the rules for distributing surplus food. The attempt then was to combine food distribution with community-promoting activities. It was thought that organising communal meals would promote the activeness of those resorting to food aid.

> 'For us, waste food is a tool, a product to be put to beneficial use by increasing a sense of community. And so, together with the network we were part of, we thought what kind of actions would promote this; how this food waste could be used to increase communal activities.' (A co-operative manager between the city and civil society)

Even though in this context one cannot talk about community economy, church social work had anyway an ambition to build the local community. This was exceptional in the sense that previously, food waste had only ever been aid for low income households, organised as a unidirectional act of handing it over to the poor by retailers and charities (Silvasti and Riches 2014). Yet from the early 2000s onwards, civic values began to be integrated with it. It was thought that surplus food could be used to promote a sense of community and participation amongst people in difficult situations. In this way, efforts were made to find a tolerable way to alleviate problems caused by poverty and loneliness in the spirit of social work, using an empowering social-pedagogical approach. Yet this new form of food aid activity was led mainly by professionals, without the powerful initiative of the beneficiaries.

> 'Our starting point for developing civic activities was that they should be empowering and involve doing things together. So this approach could mean, for example, that young men come here because they didn't get that job which they wanted, but they still want to be somehow really involved in things and learn new stuff, not just lie around at home or go to the gym. It somehow seems that they come here to argue

5 – Commoning surplus food in Finland

with us. So this is pretty difficult work, it tests what you can cope with.' (A church social worker)

When the new, communally-focused approach had been functioning for several years and information about it started to enter the wider social discussion, social sector developers discovered the use of food aid as a platform. Of course, social workers in the more pioneering municipalities had already started earlier on to work with those in the breadlines.

Up to that point, the welfare state had quietly accepted food aid: while social workers directed income support recipients towards foodbanks, albeit against the official instructions given by welfare state institutions, the state did not want to recognise foodbanks as a welfare state institution. When food aid as a platform was discovered, concerns were expressed about the underprivileged and disadvantaged people being out of reach of public services. Free food was believed to attract such people to join communal meals, then further guidance could be given to many of them to access services they had need of, such as mental health care or detoxification. In 2018, food aid actually made it into political documents. A report on inequality expressed the matter in the following way:

> 'Food aid activities will be reformed so as to target those in particular need of support. The goal of the participatory-communities-based model is to reach the most vulnerable, assess their income transfers and services, and promote participation by offering opportunities for activities that maintain their ability to function.' (Prime Minister's Office Finland 2018, 61)

Along the way, the discourse shifted from community to participation. The word 'participation' provoked discussion in which it was interpreted as referring to conditional food aid, so that no food aid would be obtained without participation in a communal meal. This was passionately opposed by the recipients of food aid and by traditional charities arranging food aid. The opposition seemed to be stronger in the political left than the political right. At the same time, state and municipal representatives denied having had aims of making food aid conditional. Instead, they stated that the aim was to both reduce the stigma associated with food aid and to make services more accessible.

When civil society groups invented new and original activities around food aid, the welfare state begun to want to incorporate these activities into its permanent mode of operation. This can be seen as the original activities of a civic society being institutionalized – hijacked as part of the system – and losing their commons-like and original nature. Communal meals can be interpreted as a commons fix – a promising practice which covers up the deficiencies of the welfare state.

Food aid recipients taking a more active role
The general and implicit norm is that food surplus belongs to low-income individuals and to the underprivileged. Help can be obtained from foodbanks through which, for example, severely indebted people who are trying to maintain their creditworthiness can keep hunger at bay: income allowance is not provided for these kinds of situations. The food bank thus offers material support when the bureaucracy is unable to do it.

A 'need' or 'low income' as principles for distributing resources are ambiguous categories. How does one define need or low income? Opinions on this matter are divided. One food aid recipient would exclude those who own their apartment outside of deserving food aid. Another pondered that the surrounding society is wealthier than ever before, and reasonable minimum living standards are constantly discussed. Low-income individuals should be able to afford traveling abroad or eating in restaurants, like the majority of members of the society do. Resorting to food aid as a way of saving money is criticised, whereas others consider it to be an acceptable practice:

> 'I live on a low income. By visiting the foodbanks, I can save enough so that I can go on holiday, for example. Or to a restaurant. Who says that someone on income allowance shouldn't go on holiday or eat out? It can easily be €30 or €40 that is needed to eat in a restaurant. If you go to an alright restaurant. And so, because I have the time, I go to the breadline. There you can get the basic foodstuffs so that you only need to buy some extra stuff from the shop. And then you can do something fun with the money saved.' (A food aid recipient)

Other conditions for receiving food aid can be observed. They may turn food aid from aid to a part of the market economy. First, some religious communities may require participation in a communal prayer. This is not, however, a stringent condition. One organisation attempted to show cultural sensitivity by excluding people in Islamic clothing from the requirement to participate in prayer, even though non-religious people were expected to participate.

Further, intoxicated people can be turned away from foodbanks. Them not being accepted is argued on moral grounds, or by appealing to safety reasons. There is fear towards the intoxicated, and they are even believed to be a concrete danger. Not everyone in breadlines agrees on this. One food aid recipient wondered that if the purpose is to distribute food to those who need it the most: why are the most needy excluded?

Surplus food has primarily alleviated income problems that are due to insufficient government support. Charities have stepped in as a partial replacement of social security. Only recently the welfare state institutions were given a stronger role than before, due to the realization that food aid could be used as a platform for bringing the underprivileged and disadvantaged together (see Prime Minister's Office Finland 2018, 61). This was interpreted as aims at activation.

Flirtations with activation measures made by public sector actors put a whole range of other actors, particularly food aid recipients, on edge. It begins to threaten both the autonomy of low-income individuals – in this case specifically their freedom to seek food aid – and also the place of charities in the overall food distribution system.

Food aid is not primarily regulated by legislation, but instead the rules associated with it are formed through daily practices, as is normally the case with commons. Foodbanks form *ad hoc* associative relationships (see Reimer 2004) and temporary community economies. People in breadlines know each other's motives for coming there, yet they often remain strangers to each other. However, when it was proposed, that foodbanks would be replaced at least partially with communal meals, the breadline community came together to defend their unconditional and free access to surplus.

This process exploded particularly in poverty-related social media groups in the internet. People resorting to food aid managed to argue why communal meals would be a worse alternative than getting a food bag, for example to those with families or those with fear of social situations. Resorting to food aid in itself meant the diminishing of individual freedom, because poor people are not free to choose what they have for food. Communal meals would diminish freedom even more, as the poor person could no longer even choose where they feed themselves.

Soon after this, the city of Helsinki gathered views from the breadline community. The concern over abolishing foodbanks and the demand to maintain them was repeatedly observed. The message of the food aid recipients was: 'It is not inhumane to stand in line.' The report explains:

5 – Commoning surplus food in Finland

'The observations of a social worker with over six years' experience of breadlines, customer discussions, and the now completed customer interviews reinforce the view that the demand to abolish traditional breadlines has not been borne out of customers' needs nor is it their will – on the contrary. The message from the people in breadlines is strong and undisputed: foodbanks need to be maintained. Certainly it is possible and there is reason to develop other ways to help as well, but there is a desire that food aid remains as is.' (Tanska 2018, 5.)

The discussion was so heated that those suggesting communal meals changed their minds or qualified already given statements.

All in all, surplus food activated people and created a commons, though not in the way that the public sector actors would have imagined. Instead, food aid beneficiaries took for themselves the space and authority to define who surplus food belongs to. This activeness was generated by the recipients of food aid from their own interests and was awakened once other actors threatened the practices which favoured the recipients, namely the unregulated food aid.

Yet, interestingly, people in breadlines suggested rules that would generate hierarchies in presenting that families with children, pensioners, students and disabled people should have separate times for distributing food to them. When food aid recipients were asked, they had the idea that alcoholics and homeless people would benefit from communal dining. (Tanska 2018, 6, 18.)

Food aid is often regarded as necessary because the welfare state has failed to sufficiently equalise incomes (see Silvasti and Riches 2014, 196). However, this statement is no longer without its cracks. Not even all food aid recipients subscribe to that statement. One social worker gave the following reflection:

'I don't really believe in it. That is, it rather bothers me sometimes that it is used more as a political drum to beat, by saying something along the lines that food aid is a sign of the deterioration of the welfare state – because there are foodbanks, and they will never disappear, and poverty itself has become something permanent. Okay, that is probably part of it, but I don't really believe it. Even if the basic level of support was raised, then where does the line go? So that no one would need to go to the breadline or food bank. Because if we assume, as is now the case, that it's pretty uncontrolled, then anyone can go there, and I myself believe that people would then continue to go there.' (A social worker)

As long as there is surplus inherent in a market economy, it will be distributed, one way or another. In the following section we show that in addition to retailers, charities, welfare state institutions, and food aid beneficiaries, surplus food has activated citizens that are not dependent on food aid, and who by using all means necessary want to get rid of the stigma associated with receiving food surplus.

Food surplus activists as entrants in the field of surplus food

The more groups operate in the area of surplus food as a commons, each with their own starting points, the more complicated the practices become. The latest entrants into this arena have been climate activists, who have set themselves the objective of breaking up the traditional alliances of charities and markets.

In 2017, a group of individual citizens established a so-called community fridge with the motive of using surplus food to mitigate climate change by increasing appreciation for food and changing consumption habits. The fridge is like a community member that gathers people around it, like an activist described the idea of the community fridge. The group of activists have agreements to collect surplus food from their collaborators on a regular basis. Food from the fridge is open to anyone who is willing to take and eat. Volunteers take care of cleaning the fridge regularly.

These newcomer actors – commoners in the sense that they aim to create spaces and activities beyond capitalism – refuse to talk about food aid. Instead, they prefer to talk about 'inclusive food', which is what they would like surplus food to be. Through this conceptual choice, they hope to influence the unwritten vernacular rules according to which surplus exclusively belongs to the poor. Inclusive surplus food, in turn, would not involve any indication of status, nor would it be socially stigmatising. The founder of the communal fridge describes it as follows:

> 'Food aid speaks so strongly of social inequality – it is profiled as something which is done for the poor. For the less-well-off. And that's why we want to be open to everyone, because here the point is that if we profile this…that's why we also want to show that this isn't some dingy cupboard in a corner somewhere but something that looks clean and tidy. Precisely so that others, that everyone would dare to come along and that it wouldn't be something scary. Because if we talk about dumpster diving for example, then that is something which is really scary to the average person. Eating food from a rubbish bin? Hell no.' (A surplus food activist)

New commoners have introduced a new agenda of negotiating, for whom surplus belongs to. They also emphasize the communal fridge as an actor in itself, bringing together residents in a particular area and connecting them with each other. Activists told that the surplus fridge binds together different social relationships, forming a common goal which people from different cultures and value systems commit to.

Behind the agenda of inclusive food is the idea that, from the climate perspective, waste food should not be considered as any less a valuable form of food. The community fridge organisers explicate that managing surplus food cannot be simply left as the responsibility of low-income individuals and food aid. Making food surplus initiatives inclusive would involve different kinds of people, increase awareness about surplus food and climate change in a positive way, would make unsustainable consumption habits visible, and create a sense of togetherness.

> 'It would be great if high income earners would also get involved, people that have jobs. And then that social label, that unpleasant stigma attached to these activities would disappear altogether.' (An inclusive food activist)

However, the emergence of these new commoners, who emphasize inclusive surplus food, has caused confusion. Both the recipients and providers of food aid are afraid that surplus food will run out and not be available for poor people any more. Food surplus activists deny these kinds of accusations, and emphasize that they are primarily aiming at raising the value of food, irrespective of the person who uses it:

> 'Is one person's mouth better than another's? What I mean is, who do we consider to be better? Because we are perhaps so fixated on that idea. We want to raise the value of food. We don't want our shelves to just get filled up with some empty cardboard boxes that look untidy. When it looks clean and tidy, then the fears associated with surplus food decrease.' (A surplus food activist)

There are signals that raising the value of food surplus seems to work as expected. For instance, some low-income individuals have embraced an eco-friendly identity, even if this actually was a *de facto* situation rather than a freedom of choice on their part. Commons and being a commoner may mitigate the social and psychic burden resulting from financial scarcity. This kind of 'involuntary eco-friendly behaviour' – which includes making use of second-hand clothing and surplus food – provides an opportunity to shift from the underprivileged margin into the sphere of recognized citizens.

Conclusions

Various actors are involved in defining the practices around food surplus as a commons and negotiating the rule of using it and the role of the different users. These actors include retailers, food aid recipients, the civil society, churches, charity organisations, the public sector actors, and climate activists.

The transformation of a good or service that is produced within a market economy into a common, brings with it challenges that need to be addressed. Food surplus, albeit unsalable in some circumstances, has use value. Charity has hijacked surplus for a good cause, when handing out food to the poor. Charity organisations are controlling both a tangible asset (the food) and an intangible asset (the right to distribute it). They are also given a monopolistic or rather restrictive trade practice by the state. This is in the case of Finland as the Churches are largely given this privilege and private people are not. Charity rarely is altruistic. Together with retailers, it creates a social node through which they both can build a brand that symbiotically benefits them both. For poor people, in turn, surplus food is a commons governed by charities. It increases one's individual well-being when the market economy and the welfare state fail to provide it. Even though foodbanks do not create a permanent community economy, they nevertheless create temporary economies, spaces for exchanging peer support, knowledge and tips. In this way, they function as a communal platform. Surplus is also more and more utilised as a resource for increasing climate awareness, as food surplus activists make visible the unsustainability of consumerism and overproduction. Tensions arise when these kinds of movements threaten the position of others.

The first chapter of this book presented three alternative attitudes a welfare state can take towards community economies. We can apply these alternatives – inaction, direct assistance and institutional learning, and creating enabling background conditions – to surplus as a commons.

It is evident that if there is a desire to secure the principles of the Nordic welfare state, pure inaction is out of the question, as the market threatens the principles of the Nordic welfare state. As a consequence of indifference, an increased emphasis on individual responsibility and the break-up of state-commons can be expected.

However, the welfare state institutions can learn from civil society actors. The Finnish welfare state has already learned how to utilise surplus food as an incentive that brings together people who are in a vulnerable position. It is acknowledged that charity organisations and civil society movements operate at the grassroot level, which makes them more capable of reaching people with difficulties. In this sense, surplus food serves as 'a complementary welfare service' at the intersections of civil society, charity and the public sector. However, the alliance of the welfare state, market economy and charity appears to be complicated. It may accelerate the processes deteriorating the universalistic basis of the welfare state. What would be compatible with the universalistic ethos of the Nordic welfare state is that economic activity having to do with all sorts of surplus would build community economies, where people regardless of social class would join and generate social value. Food surplus as a commons has the potential to transform from poverty-targeted foodbanks into more permanent community economies and commoning. This way food surplus as a commons may work as a platform for community democracy development and have an empowering function. Participating in managing the commons – e.g. through deliberative negotiations about who is included or excluded from surplus food as a resource – may direct agency towards activities with aims to change the state of affairs.

5 – Commoning surplus food in Finland

Although Finnish welfare state institutions and climate activists have not yet come closely together as actors, they would have opportunities to create a sort of 'commons fix' that benefits all people. If it were to become more widespread, community activities around surplus food is a mode of operation that has the potential to challenge the unsustainable market economy. There are traits attached to the activity of food surplus and climate change that indicate the possibilities for emerging community economies where new social values, such as the sense of meaningfulness and worth, are created in collaboration with local residents. Food aid indeed makes the everyday life of people of low income easier, but in addition to this, in some circumstances it seems to attract activity that unites people of different socio-economic groups locally. Instead of using food surplus only as a means of guiding the underprivileged to services that they are paternalistically evaluated to be in need of, the welfare institutions could create enabling conditions for local cohesion to develop through community economies too.

When it comes to surplus as a commons, a strict division, which separates the welfare state as the public arena, the market and charity as the private arena and the civil society somewhere in between as the third sector, is not necessarily sound. This type of strict division would easily lead to antiquated ways to examine the surplus, for instance, as either waste or food aid. If the climate issue that is a shared problem across the world is not taken into consideration, no new views for solutions are opened. Surplus food is very much a common issue, where its control and negotiations having to do with controlling it belong to all. In other words, surplus food is a commons within the common – and it may be a force that arranges being and acting locally, nationally and globally. It may play a role as a challenger that forces the welfare state and the market economy to reform.

Once having emerged, no one can know for sure the role that the commons will end up taking – whether they will become servants of the dominant economic system or band aids to patch up the deficiencies of the welfare state (see De Angelis 2013). They can become something used for unduly maintaining the triad of the welfare state, charities, and capitalism. They can form a symbiotic relationship with some or all of these three. Or they can form a system that acts as an agent of change.

6
Self-organised online ridesharing as a 'transport commons'

Juhana Venäläinen

During the last five years, Facebook-based ridesharing has gained popularity as a way of coordinating shared car trips from one city to another. Amid the widespread hype and political expectations around 'the sharing economy' (e.g. Sundararajan 2016; John 2017) and 'the platform economy' (e.g. Parker et al. 2016), this model of shared mobility stands out as strikingly homespun. While commercial services such as Uber are slowly gaining ground as an alternative for short-distance trips, there are few commercial services to date in Finland for individuals wishing to share a car for a longer journey. Thus, the self-made alternative that utilises Facebook as a noticeboard poses an attractive alternative for passengers seeking the cheapest way of getting around within the country, or for drivers seeking persons to split their fuel costs. On top of the economic benefits, ridesharing offers the possibility to meet interesting people, have someone to chat with, and to promote ecological values.

Ridesharing has also become topical because of the rising awareness of the drastic changes needed to tackle climate change in the transport sector in wealthy welfare states. In governmental reports, ridesharing is mentioned as an example of the emerging 'sustainable travel services' that are expected to provide alternatives to owning and driving a private car (e.g. MoTC 2018b). In this respect, the case for self-organised ridesharing is interesting not only because of its current and potential role in the travel system, but also as a broader *cultural form* that enacts ideas about reconfiguring the relation between individually and collectively oriented mobility practices. While being a more social way of travel than driving alone, ridesharing bears an ethos of individualism and self-reliance, which sets it far apart from the 'traditional' modes of public transportation.

In this chapter, I will analyse whether, in which sense, under what conditions and to what extent the formation of self-organised ridesharing could be understood as a *transport commons* that challenges and transforms the former role of the welfare state in coordinating and overseeing public transport. I understand the transport commons not as a mere pool of 'resources', but an assemblage of social practices, common objectives, culturally shared values and material constituents required for pursuing a particular task: in this case, the task of getting from one place to another. As David Bollier (2011) writes, 'a commons arises whenever a given community decides that it wishes to manage a resource in a collective manner, with a special regard for equitable access, use and sustainability'. While online self-organised ridesharing, in some senses, is a very illustrative example of a commons, it also has characteristics that do not easily fit into Bollier's definition and could even lead to questioning whether it makes sense to use the term or not. For example: Is there a 'community' that has intentionally 'decided' something? Or, how 'collective' or 'collectively managed' are the privately-owned cars used in the practice? And, last but not least, how important are 'equitable access' or 'sustainability' as values motivating the practice?

Commons-based peer production (Benkler 2006; Papadimitropoulos 2018) has been proposed as a way to transcend the dichotomy between the market and the state in providing essential services (e.g. Bollier and Helfrich 2013). Building upon the overarching topic of this volume, here I examine how the model of self-organised ridesharing systemically relates to the roles of the state and commercial entities in providing transport options. In the analysis, I will highlight the conditions, potentials and tensions of ridesharing vis-à-vis the responsibilities of the welfare state in providing a sort of 'backstop' of mobility services that ought to be equally accessible to everyone throughout the country. I will also debate the ambivalent ecological implications of ridesharing. The analysis is informed by ongoing research on the Finnish ridesharing system as an 'interface' to the debates about the sharing economy and its political connotations. The research utilises both qualitative and quantitative data, including statistical data about the ridesharing groups, individual conversation threads, and an online survey.[17]

The emergence of self-organised ridesharing in Finland
Ridesharing is a phenomenon with multiple social and cultural histories. From the perspective of transport alone, it is a contemporary variation of the age-old practice of travelling together. A different view is that ridesharing in its current online-mediated form is a relatively recent and a qualitatively distinct phenomenon that was only rendered possible after the breakthrough of digital technology, global communications networks, social media, and the online peer-to-peer marketplaces as a socio-cultural form.

In the course of history, different political contexts as well as different technological innovations have given shape to ridesharing (Chan and Shaheen 2012). Even in a particular moment, there are myriad reasons and forms of the practice. For example, taking

---

17 The research was carried out as part of the project 'Rights, excludability and the social production of value in the models of the new economy', funded by the Kone Foundation 2016–2018.

a neighbour's kid to a hobby is a common type of *informal rideshraring*. Commuting rideshares, for their part, are typically based on continuous, contractual arrangements. The subset of ridesharing analysed in this chapter is slightly different: the trips are occasional, and the most common purpose is to visit a friend or a relative who lives in another city.

In Finland, the history of online ridesharing dates back to the early 2000s, when the first website for ridesharing was established by an individual who wanted to find people to share driving expenses (Helsingin Uutiset 2010). Two decades later, Facebook has become the leading platform for organising long-distance peer-to-peer ridesharing in Finland, with about 160 independent ridesharing groups and an estimated total member count around 100,000 (ca. 2% of the Finnish population).[18] The reason for the popularity of Facebook as a noticeboard for ridesharing is obvious: with the massive user base and the fact that many people have learned to organise various aspects of their social lives through social media, it is much easier to find one's way to ridesharing there rather than by browsing on a separate website.

An essential contextual factor for understanding long-distance ridesharing in Finland is that the distances between major cities in Finland are rather long. For example, the distance between Oulu (the fifth largest city) and Helsinki (the capital) is about 600 kilometres, which means an approximately seven-hour drive. Journeys of this scale, with the associated fuel costs, offer a tempting

---

18 The cumulative member count for all the groups analysed was 250,000, but clearly, there is a substantial overlap between the groups, i.e. that one person belonging to more than one group. In the survey conducted, respondents reported being a member of 2.5 groups on average. Thus, using this figure would lead to the estimate of 100,000 unique members, but as the survey was self-selected, it is likely that the survey sample represents the more-than-averagely active users who would also belong to more groups than an average user. Another point to consider is that only a relatively small part of the membership is active in the sense of posting ride announcements. In a sample of 7,281 posts analysed from a medium-large group, only 26% of the members had posted something within the last year.

incentive to split travel costs through ridesharing. Typically, a ridetaker pays a small fee, from 5 to 20 euros. While not a pure gift, the arrangement is still a win-win situation: the passenger gets an affordable ride, and the driver gets an opportunity to reduce their driving expenses.

Whereas the main routes like Helsinki–Oulu are also well served by trains, buses and flights, ridesharing serves a slightly different purpose in routes where public transport options are limited – for example in the 'transverse' itineraries from eastern to western parts of the country, or the routes in the sparsely populated areas in northern Finland. There, the role of ridesharing is not so much to compete on price but to offer a complementary travel option to driving one's own car for the ones who do not have a car, and for routes where there are few public transport options available.

Globally, the 'secondary market' (Benkler 2004) of ridesharing has invited so-called sharing economy businesses to create commercial platforms to facilitate the exchange. Mobile app based BlaBlaCar, for example, operates in 22 countries and has more than 35 million members, and has turned ridesharing into a 'multi-million-euro business', charging a service fee between 10–34% of the price of the ride (Cowan 2015). So far, BlaBlaCar or other major ridesharing services have not begun to operate in Finland, which has left room for the self-organised alternatives.

In contrast to commercial ridesharing services, the Facebook-based ridesharing groups have been established and are maintained by voluntary moderators who do not seek financial gain. A ridesharing group for a particular route or area is born when someone feels the urge for such a forum to exist and is motivated enough to establish one. Those groups that reach the critical mass to become a feasible noticeboard grow into much more than the personal projects of their establishers: they become institutions and *de facto* monopolies for coordinating the rides for a specific geographical location.

The spontaneously born quality of the groups is reflected in their geographically dispersed structure. Although there is also a relatively large nation-wide ridesharing group (ca. 50,000 members), it is often more convenient and effective to post an announcement to a local group instead. This dispersed group structure contributes to the organisational resilience of the system: even if one group closed down, this would not threaten the ridesharing system as a whole, as there would be an opportunity for another group to occupy its role.

Ridesharing as a commons?
When the ridesharing groups are conceived as a whole, they can be depicted as a system where the individual and relatively autonomous groups together constitute a whole 'transport commons'. A *commons system* is a social arrangement where resources (here, the car seats) are pooled and redistributed in a self-organising process. Analytically, the notion of a commons system brings together material assets (cars, roads, means of communication), people (the ones offering rides and the ones looking for them) and the particular practices of *commoning* 'through which commonwealth and the community of commoners are (re)produced together with the (re)production of stuff, social relations, affects, decisions, cultures' (De Angelis 2017, 119).

There are, however, several aspects which quite fundamentally question the status of ridesharing as a form of 'commoning'. First of all, if commons are understood in terms of *decommodification*, it is disturbing to observe how prominent a role money plays in the practice: for a large majority of the rides, at least something is expected to be paid; and for a large majority of the people involved, paying for a ride is self-evident.[19] The idea of paying for

---

19 In the survey data, only 8% reported that they did not pay anything for the last ride; 42% paid 10 euros (n=271). When asking explicitly about the understandings of a just price, only 8% selected the option ridesharing is about helping others out – money is secondary, whereas the 92% chose options suggesting that at least something should be paid for a ride (n=370).

a journey is not surprising if ridesharing is compared to taking a bus or a train, but if it is compared to hitch-hiking or other more informal types of shared mobility, it might actually appear as commodifying the conventions of mutual aid rather than enlarging the non-commodified space.

Secondly, the deep reliance on a commercial platform – Facebook – makes ridesharing vulnerable in many ways. It is uncertain whether the platform will retain its popularity and whether it will have similar functions in the future to support self-organised exchange. On the other hand, depending on a platform whose profit logic is based on capitalizing social exchange through targeted advertising (Fuchs 2012) does not fit easily to the notion of building collective practices outside of the capitalist market.

Thirdly, the communal aspect of ridesharing – the *sense of community*, but also the concrete social practices related to commoning – is somewhat thin and tends to be a form of a dyadic, contractual relationship between the 'buyer' and the 'seller'. This is reflected, for example, in the widespread understanding that negotiating a fair price for a ride is a 'private affair' between the two counterparts,[20] and also in the explicit and implicit codes of conduct in the groups that strongly discourage any 'political' debates about pricing. Evidently, also the fact that the ridesharing system is completely dependent on *private* cars owned and managed by *individuals* renders it dubious from the perspectives of equity and inclusiveness, as there are no effective means for the 'community' to collectively decide about the use of resources.

Fourthly, the conditions of reproduction and resilience of this system are precarious and devoid of planned safeguarding mechanisms. To be sure, the dispersed group structure is an advantage from the viewpoint of resilience, but still, the system

---

20   'What is your opinion about these arguments related to the price of a shared ride: Negotiating about the price is a private affair between the ridegiver and the ridetaker: 58% completely agree, 31% somewhat agree.

as a whole could be easily disrupted by even a minor change in the terms and conditions of the platform or the regulative environment, not to mention the possibility of a commercial ridesharing operator conquering the field. The lack of common commitment or a well-articulated common objective – which in a way is a natural consequence of the much underlined 'practical' and individualistic character of the practice – leaves the system vulnerable to various kinds of internal and external perturbations. Further, from the perspective of ecological reproduction, the strong reliance on private cars, mostly fossil fuel-powered, is a short-sighted solution, as tackling climate change would require a rapid transition towards net emissions-free traffic modes.

In the discussions about the commons, there is sometimes a tendency to idealise their self-governance and, vice-versa, to downplay the ways in which they depend on and interact with the 'non-common' social systems (see Lund and Venäläinen 2016). The commons of ridesharing, while being spontaneously born, self-organised and self-managed, are far from being completely *autonomous*. Rather, they rely in manifold ways on the resources of the state, market, and household actors (Figure 1). However, ridesharing can still challenge the formal transport system, or at least the ways how we *think* about transport, by introducing an alternative organisational logic and incubating alternative notions of 'value' (see Chapter 2).

6 – Self-organised online ridesharing as a 'transport commons'

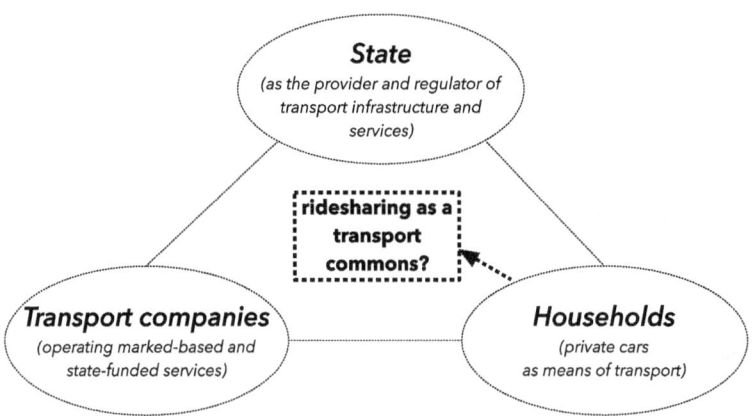

Figure 1. The operating space for ridesharing as a commons.

The tendency of commodification

> 'After begging, hitching is the most elementary point of contact between those who have and those who have not. It is a basic exchange between need and ability to provide.' (Perkins 2016)

In a column for *The Guardian*, journalist Anne Perkins laments the decline of hitch-hiking as a 'modern tragedy'. Hitching depended, she writes, 'on a sense of solidarity, and the sense of trust and mutuality', but also on serendipity, 'the happy accident of the unexpected place or person', which in the current form of ridesharing has been reduced into dull predictability. (Perkins 2016.) These affective encounters – the 'happy accidents', unexpectedness, and the senses of togetherness – at least partly explain why hitch-hiking once was popular even in a welfare state like Finland. In hitch-hiking, there is an 'excess of exchange'

(Eskelinen and Venäläinen forthcoming) that goes far beyond the bare calculative rationality of measuring euros against the distance travelled.

Hitch-hiking and ridesharing bear some interesting similarities and differences. Exactly like hitching, ridesharing fosters non-market practices for fulfilling elementary mobility needs but – in contrast to some other forms of community economies – mostly without an explicit ethical or political agenda. Instead, sharing is motivated and explicated by the notion that it is simply 'reasonable' to harness the surplus capacity of cars. This sort of 'reasonableness', which seems to counterpoint the spontaneous and unpredictable character of hitching, may be seen as a step towards the commodification of mutual aid into 'services' that need to be compensated by paying the price.

While the informal ridesharing practices such as hitch-hiking, travelling with a family member or taking a neighbour's kid to football training are typically based on the logic of a unilateral gift (see Mikołajewska-Zając 2016), ridesharing and even its self-organised subtype leans heavily towards the logic of the market: selling and buying, asking for a price, negotiating about the price, and finally making a monetary transaction or withdrawing from it. What this kind of commodification implies is that a person who is not able or willing to pay the price would be excluded from this commons.

Anthropologist David Graeber (2014) argues that even the notion of the gift conceals three 'fundamentally different moral logics' or 'categories of economic transaction' that can be found in every society, including the one in a welfare state: hierarchy, communism, and exchange. These logics operate closely together, and even in a single occasion of economic reasoning, people might resort to multiple (and potentially conflicting) combinations.

Hierarchy and communism are both based on the notion of giving a gift without expecting anything specific in return. The difference between the two is that hierarchy, such as a charity donation, assumes and establishes an unequal and asymmetric relation between those helping and those receiving help. In contrast, communism subscribes to a strong understanding of mutuality: a sort of permanent 'indebtedness' of everyone to everyone.

The logic of exchange differs from hierarchy and communism in its pertinent strive for commensurability and equivalence. Within the logic of exchange, a gift should be always counterbalanced by an equally valuable counter-gift now or later. Consequently, there can be no real gifts, since they only appear as transitory moments in the endless cycle of credit and debit.

Graeber's analysis shows that the introduction of money as such does not determine how 'commercial' or 'non-commercial' a practice is. Giving money to someone implies different things in different contexts: not all economic forms involving money are commodified, nor do all commodified activities involve the use of currency as a medium. Thus, it is important to examine how the economic activity is discursively framed both in the self-understandings of the participants and in the socio technical structures and cultural forms sustaining the cooperation, but also how the price as a barrier of entry to the service includes some persons and excludes others from using the commons.

Yochai Benkler (2004) notes that 'social systems of sharing' are categorically different from 'secondary markets'. While secondary markets rely mostly on the price mechanism in redistributing the surplus capacity of a system, sharing systems are more deeply intertwined with the 'tacit, learned, and culturally reproduced capacities to read and interpret social settings' (ibid., 304). In commons-based sharing, price may play some role, but it typically is not a factor that dominates the practices of exchange or determines the access to resources. Ridesharing, in the context of this dichotomy, has properties from both worlds: it is not *only* an ordinary marketplace, as the conceptions of about the role of money are more varying and complex than in an ordinary market transaction, but it is *also* an ordinary marketplace, and ever more often so, which is exemplified by that fact that many groups today allow selling and buying train and bus tickets as well as organising shared rides, thus positing ridesharing as a just another marketised travel mode among others.

A commons system or a 'commons fix'?
Ridesharing, as well as any other form of commoning in a welfare state context, is at a continuous risk of becoming a commons fix: a source of ideological justification for the privatisation of public services. Throughout Europe, public services that were once established as part of the welfare state regime are first being pushed into the logic of new public management, and then gradually privatised or semi-privatised (see Introduction). This transformation comes along with a discourse that stresses factors such as 'diversity of producers' and the role of the third sector.

The discourse of 'freedom of choice' has populated the political spectrum in many sectors from health care to family policy. The implicit criticism embedded in this discourse is that in providing public services, the welfare state has been too paternalistic and rigid, imposing a top-down view on what its citizens need instead of actually listening to their varied wishes. The concrete conclusion for implementing this 'freedom of choice' is then to increase the role of businesses and other private entities in service provision by outsourcing tasks and opening markets. This process of 'diversifying' service production might entail quite different outcomes in different regions. In the context of transport, those living in bigger cities and densely populated areas already have more 'freedom of choice' between the different ways to travel, whereas the ones living in more sparsely populated areas tend to feel that they have no choice to having and driving a car.

Examining ridesharing in the context of a welfare state might easily bring about a tacit assumption that the role of ridesharing in relation to the state and market would be uniform throughout

6 – Self-organised online ridesharing as a 'transport commons'

the country. However, both the survey data and the quantitative analysis of the group structure lead to a conclusion that from a functional perspective, there is not a single system of online ridesharing in Finland, but actually two slightly different constellations that reflect the different economic-geographical circumstances in different parts of the country (see Figure 2). Roughly put, the ridesharing groups in the sparsely populated areas of eastern and northern Finland seem to be born out of a very practical necessity – as a way of *getting around* and *getting by* in the first place –, whereas the groups serving the southern routes are more directly competing with the existing public transport options.

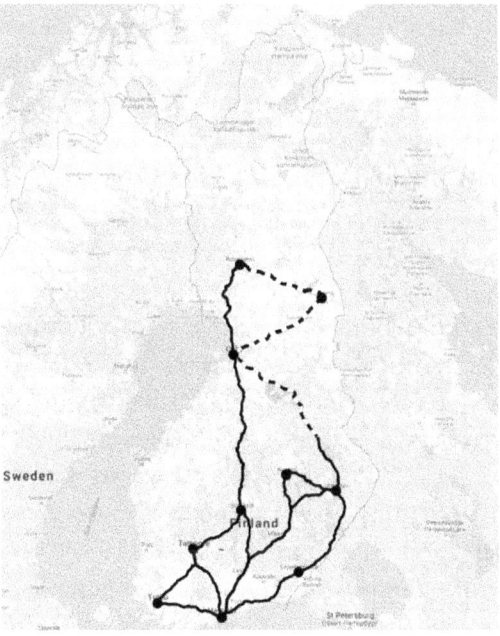

Figure 2.   *Estimate of the ten most popular ridesharing routes based on the groups' member counts. Dashed line routes are scarcely served by public transport. Base map: Google Maps.*

In northern and eastern Finland, the distances between major cities are typically in the range of hundreds of kilometres. While there typically are a couple of bus connections per day between most cities, the offerings can be quite limited, lengthy in terms of travel time, and even relatively expensive in comparison to driving a car. These circumstances have been fruitful for the emergence of ridesharing groups: of the 20 largest ridesharing groups, 7 are situated in these sparsely inhabited regions.

In the more densely populated southern Finland, many of the popular ridesharing groups target the same high-traffic main routes that are also operated by bus companies, some routes also having frequent train connections. In those situations, the function of ridesharing is very different in comparison to the northern/eastern context: it might either push down the price even further than the low-cost bus lines, or it might partly attract people who prefer the experience of ridesharing in comparison to riding a bus.

Neither of the constellations gives the impression of ridesharing functioning solely as a 'commons fix' that would justify the under-supply of public transport or legitimise the withdrawal of the welfare state from safeguarding essential mobility services. In the northern/eastern context, a flexible transport system such as ridesharing may actually be a relatively efficient and convenient solution in comparison to the scarce supply and fixed schedules of the public transport options, whereas in the south the flows of traffic are so high that it is unlikely for a distributed practice like ridesharing to actually compete with the public transport to any significant extent. However, between the two polarities there is a large area of borderline cases: for example, routes and places where a functional public transport would be realistic to provide but lacks operators, funding, and political support, and also routes where the public transport options are already reasonably good, yet where sharing a car is still *conceived* to be more affordable, convenient or otherwise desirable than travelling by bus or a train.

The systemic risk of commons-based ridesharing compensating

6 – Self-organised online ridesharing as a 'transport commons'

for insufficient public transport infrastructure is problematic not only in terms of regional policy but also in terms of constitutional rights. The 'right to choose one's place of residence' as defined in the Finnish constitution is not only a negative right (i.e., that the government should not restrict a person's choice of place of residence) but also implies that public authorities should 'implement positive measures through which the choice actually becomes possible' (Government proposal to the Parliament on the amend the Fundamental Rights Regulation of the Constitution, HE 309/1993 vp., 51, translated here).

The constitutional rights' perspective exemplifies the stark contrast between the logic of public service provision and the one of peer-to-peer provision: in the latter, there is no way to require nor a reason to expect any specific service form to prosper, as the arrangement is based on spontaneous voluntarily cooperation, the longevity of which rests on multiple precarious factors: the personal motivation of the providers, the social dynamics of the sharing community, the conditions imposed by the platform(s), along with other technological necessities, the regulative framework imposed by the governmental, transnational and local actors, etc. A service functioning well today can break down tomorrow, or gradually decline without anyone taking responsibility for the change of course.

In addition to doubts over longevity, another aspect that sets the public services apart from peer provision is their universalism: the premise of offering a service to everyone entitled to it. Public service provision is based on the requirement to serve all customers, so no discrimination between difficult and easy customers can be made, whereas the peer-to-peer model exemplified by ridesharing relies on the ability of the counterparts to reach an agreement, as well as having an adequate social ranking and reputation within the platform (see Hearn 2010). It is indeed a strange paradox that the peer economies are so often portrayed as embracing 'communal values', while in fact they may promote an extremely individualistic and excluding political ontology: a survival of the fittest (or popular) where the different forms of structural discrimination are being swept under the rug of 'personal preference'. This stems from the notion that sharing a personal space – such as one's car – still leaves all control to its owner rather than the ones who participate in other roles. Even if the person seeking a ride is excluded for racial or socioeconomic discrimination, there is no way to appeal against it.

The ecological implications of carsharing
From the perspective of resource use, private car traffic is a hugely wasteful system. In Finland, the average rate of occupancy in cars is 1.7 persons, which means that only one-third of the registered seating capacity (5.1 seats per car on average) is utilised (National Travel Survey 2012; Trafi 2017). This equation sets the theoretical upper limit to how much the carbon footprint of private car traffic could be decreased by sharing: if the same amount of passengers would be transported with one third of the number of cars, as is technically possible, the greenhouse gas emissions from private car traffic would decrease from 5.9 million tons to under 2.0 million CO^2-eqv tons, a reduction of about 7% in Finland's annual greenhouse gas emissions (based on LIPASTO 2018 and Statistics Finland 2018a; calculated from 2017 figures).

Having all cars full of passengers is obviously impossible, but even a slight increase in the occupancy rate would have a notable impact on the national carbon footprint. According to the survey conducted by the author in Finnish ridesharing groups, the average distance of a ridesharing trip was 290 km, and the occupancy rate 3.1 persons per car. These figures suffice to show that ridesharing as a mobility practice could have a significant impact on reducing the overall carbon spend of the transport sector: it could supplement the decarbonisation of transport in reducing overall CO^2 emissions, if it would be upscaled to broaden the user base. This potential is tacitly expressed in a report from the Ministry of Communications and Transport that describes MaaS (Mobility as a Service), including 'shared trips', as one of the three possible pathways to a carbon-free transport system for Finland by 2045 (the other two being the use of biofuels and the shift to 'alternative driving power' such as electricity and biogas) (MoTC 2018a). However, the report also notes uncertainty over the extent, to which the novel mobility solutions will decrease car traffic, and the extent that they will compete with public transport (ibid., 43). This reservation is very important in the context of ridesharing. In effect, only 11% of the respondents in the ridesharing survey conducted for this study reported driving a car as the alternative option for their last trip if they would not have found a shared ride – whereas 52% would have taken the bus and 30% the train. A large majority of ridesharing today does not seem to substitute car driving, but rather it substitutes the (potential) use of ecologically more efficient modes of public transport. Thus, the overall ecological impacts of ridesharing are ambivalent: while ridesharing evidently increases the eco-efficiency of a single ride, it might also have contrary effects at the level of the transport *system* if it decreases the demand for public transport and increases private car traffic.

Despite the public image of ridesharing as an especially environmentally conscious form of travel, ecological motivations were not very pronounced in the survey data. In the survey, only 24% of those who had offered rides considered *environmental friendliness* as 'very significant' or 'moderately significant' factor in their decision to offer a shared ride. The share was higher amongst those who had participated in ridesharing as a passenger, yet far behind the more 'practical' motivational factors (*low price* 88%, *flexible schedules* 73%, *shorter travel time* 56%, *lack of public transport* 56%). The same pattern can be seen in the description texts of the ridesharing groups, of which only one in seven mentions environmental motivations, usually combining them with the economic ones: *'Let's travel together – saving money and nature!'* (For similar results, see Hamari et al. 2015.)

The attitudes of the people involved in ridesharing do not determine the environmental footprint of the practice, but the ideas and opinions of the ridesharers can still be considered as proxies in trying to understand the dynamics of how the travel mode is chosen. If the price of travel is at least *somewhat* important for more than 95% of the ridesharers, as suggested by the survey, then the popularity of ridesharing is extremely dependent on factors external to the ridesharing community: namely, the price of the alternative transport options and the participants' ability to pay for them. Some respondents of the survey mentioned that the increased supply of affordable bus tickets (and to a lesser extent, train tickets) had decreased the use of ridesharing, either in their own choices or in their observations more generally.

In debates about the sharing economy, it has occasionally been argued that services like Uber are sabotaging or at least disrupting the public transport system by outcompeting it with a less eco-friendly alternative (Light and Miskelly 2015; Lindsay 2017). With the current level of competition in the low-cost coach supply for the high-volume routes in Finland, this trajectory is mostly hypothetical. What is more contestable is the medium-term ecological impact of ridesharing in areas where 'there is no alternative' to owning a car: would a too strong ridesharing arrangement signal that developing public transport is not needed, as people can already cope with sharing their cars? Or would a government-issued financial incentive to promote ridesharing encourage people to shift from buses to cars rather than from solo rides to shared rides? From the perspective of a sustainable and climate-conscious welfare state, it is crucial to thoroughly assess this kind of environmental dilemma, related to alternative economic practices, and take them properly into account when devising strategies of regulation.

The insights from the ridesharing practices are useful in putting into context the prospects as to how large an extent technological change, especially the development of autonomous vehicles, help to tackle climate change. It is too often taken for granted that the domain of mobility-as-a-service will automatically decrease the environmental footprint of driving because it becomes *technically* easier to share cars, borrow them for short periods and to combine them with other modes of transport. However, these technical possibilities alone, without well-targeted incentives and regulation, do not have a strong influence on travel preferences. With the automation of car traffic, we might actually see a growing number of cars driving a growing number of kilometres: Trommer et al. (2016) estimate that the introduction of autonomous vehicles will result in a 3–9% increase in vehicle-kilometres travelled by 2035.

Decommodifying public transport
Self-organised online ridesharing can be seen as a form of peer production that challenges the traditional public transport services typical in developed welfare states as well as the more commercially oriented platforms of sharing. For ridesharing to function as a transport commons that would help to decommodify the domain of public transport, three major caveats have to be addressed. Firstly, there is a risk of 'commodification from within', it is, the users gradually assuming more and more instrumental values regarding the meanings of ridesharing, it thereby becoming just another (niche) product in the transport market. Secondly, there is the risk of ridesharing functioning as a 'commons fix' to legitimate the deterioration of state-supported mass public transport solutions that would be more equitable and environmentally-friendly than sharing a private car. Thirdly, the relevance of ridesharing as a commons system is radically limited by the ways through which it depends on 'non-common' systems (such as private cars and a corporate platform). These three aspects will be discussed in the following section.

The ubiquitous and largely unquestioned role of money in ridesharing gives an impression that even without the pressure from commercial ridesharing platforms, the model of ridesharing is already relatively commodified. The social context of operating in 'buying and selling groups'[21] creates a tacit expectation that a ride not only *may* have a price but also *should* have a price. A free ride might raise doubts in any case – like a free lunch –, but with the user interface now explicitly querying for the price tag, the user is strongly encouraged to ask for at least a few euros. Certainly, promoting a critical discourse of 'surplus resources' (such as underutilised car seats) and creating marketplaces for trading those is preferable from the perspective of resource efficiency. But while the practices of commoning might often be resource efficient, *all 'resource efficiency' is not commoning*, but even on the contrary. As commoning attempts to find ways out from the hegemonies of market valuation *and* state control, the process of creating markets for previously non-commodified things under the rubric of being 'smart' or 'resource-wise' could be even seen as enclosing the commons – limiting the access to the previously uncommodified surplus (as it still was understood in the golden era of hitch-hiking, i.e. 1960s and 1970s, see Stewart 2011). The institutionalisation of ridesharing as a 'service', however peer-produced it be, renders the practice more permeable by the conventional market logics and downplays its potential as an alternative to market-based valuation or the universalistic ethos of the welfare state. Already accepting money as an unproblematic medium to organise social relations implies that the current 'commons' or 'semicommons' of ridesharing would be difficult to defend against deepening commodification if a commercial platform with reasonable pricing and convenient user interface would enter the field.

In relation to the state-level transport politics, self-organised ridesharing poses an alternative and a challenge to established

---

21 In 2015, Facebook introduced a 'buy and sell group' feature that allows structured data such as the price asked for a product to be written in a separate field (to be presented to the user in a different colour) for group posts. Many, if not most, of the ridesharing groups adopted this new feature almost immediately.

forms of transport, and especially to public transport. It operates in the grey area and at a blind spot of the state bureaucracy, where the transactions are small enough not to arouse interest among the tax officials (cf. the case of timebanks in Chapter 2). While highlighting the potential of ridesharing, it is also crucial to pay attention to the systemic limits in the peer provision of transport services: what they can do and what they should do, but also on what they cannot do and what functions they should not take. If we take seriously the idea that ridesharing could be 'scaled up' (Utting 2015) into a significant mode of travel in some routes, there is a risk that it would render the situation of mass public transport even more difficult and contribute to a vicious circle (fewer passengers, decreasing profitability, decreasing service level, fewer passengers…). In the current scale of ridesharing, this payoff is marginal or almost invisible, but if aiming to understand the *systemic* relations of ridesharing to other social systems, its effects have to be examined from the perspective of its potential rather than its current popularity.

As a socio-material assemblage, ridesharing is dependent on three foundational infrastructures that are not available 'in common' but are predominantly organised within the economic domains of household, state and market (Table 2). Firstly, there is the pool of private cars – about 2.7 million units in use (Statistics Finland 2018b) – and their owners who decide in the first place whether they allow them for shared use, and under which conditions. Secondly, ridesharing depends on the state-regulated traffic infrastructure with the monopoly of maintaining a public road network, mandating traffic regulations and devising different tax schemes and incentives for different modes of transport. Thirdly, online ridesharing currently depends largely on the social and technological infrastructure provided by Facebook, which again is dependent on the global internet infrastructure, and all the computers and smartphones used for accessing the ridesharing groups. Ultimately, all the three infrastructures rely on the supply of ecological resources: oil, precious metals and different sources of energy. While Massimo De Angelis (2017, 122) maintains that commoning is 'an activity that develops relations preoccupied by their reproduction and [...] the 'sustainability' of the commons', it seems that the capability of the ridesharing system to reproduce itself is limited. Thus, even though the organisational model of online ridesharing boasts features like self-governance and the lack of hierarchies, its autonomy is of a very relative kind: in effect, it is in relation to the surplus or the 'waste' that the contemporary way of life – and driving cars as a part of it – produces (cf. Chapter 5).

6 – Self-organised online ridesharing as a 'transport commons'

	PRIVATE CARS	ROAD NETWORK	FACEBOOK
Economic domain	individual household	the state, municipalities, road communities	the (global) market
Type of infrastructure	stock of tools / 'means of production'	material infrastructure, repairing machines	social infrastructure
Material basis	metals, glass, rubber, synthetic fibres, electricity (for assembly)	asphalt concrete from petroleum and mineral aggregates, concrete, steel, paint	telecommunications network, data centres, electricity, users' laptops, tablets and smartphones
Scale	Finland: ca. 2.7 million cars in traffic use (2018) [1]	Finland: ca. 100 000 km of public roads (2017) [2]	Finland: ca. 2.8 million monthly active users (2018, forecast) [3]
Market value	ca. €18 bn [4]	ca. €15 bn [5]	ca. $400 bn (≈ €350 bn) [6]
Expense structure	capital costs, repairs, taxes, fuel, cleaning, vehicle fluids, insurance	maintenance and construction, ca. €0.8 bn per year (2017) [5]	maintenance and development, ca. $20 bn (€17.5 bn) per year (2017) [7]
Primary funding source(s)	personal income, savings or credit	tax revenue	targeted advertising
Profit-seeking?	mostly not	no	yes
Who can enter	owner decides	anyone (for driving a car, a person with a valid driving license)	(almost) anyone over 13 years old and registered to the service
Access fee	owner decides	free of charge (except for road tax, driving license, etc.)	free of charge
Conditions of use	owner decides	traffic regulations as specified in the Road Traffic Decree	defined in Terms of Service and several other policies

Table 2. *Underlying infrastructures of ridesharing. Sources: [1] Statistics Finland 2018b. [2] FTA 2017. [3] Statista 2018. [4] Estimated calculated from FICoAS 2018a; FICoAS 2018b and Autotalli.com 2018. [5] FTA 2018. [6] YCharts 2018. [7] Macrotrends 2018.*

Towards a public–commons partnership for promoting ridesharing

While ridesharing has several issues that severely question its eligibility to be considered as a commons system, it still has traces and 'germs' (Merten and Meretz 2008) of 'non-market' or 'alternative market' economic principles such as subsistence, care, conviviality, and the redistribution of surplus. Ridesharing not only pushes towards the commodification of mutual aid, but also towards the *commonification* of the basic services provision; and to the practical experimentation of trying to rethink, reframe and re-experience 'the economy'. For the welfare state, then, the crucial question is: How to coordinate peer production fruitfully with the public, universal service provision? Answering to this involves stepping into a logic that Michel Bauwens (2012) calls the one of a *partner state* (see Chapter 1), which would appreciate the self-determination of the ridesharers, but simultaneously fine-tune the regulation so that the peer-produced services would in the best possible way support the state's broader objectives within a specific policy sector. In transport, the objective would be to harness the massive fleet of private cars to extend the notion and the capability of public transport as much as possible without competing with the existing services.

For supporting ridesharing, it seems unlikely that the state could provide a platform that could become as popular as the self-organised but Facebook-dependent version is today. However, there are other options – from the small and immediate to the broader and strategic – as to how the public sector could form fruitful alliances with the ridesharing community and with the different schemes of peer production more generally. This would, however, require a fundamental change in the discourse that currently approaches the phenomena of sharing/platform/gig economy from a relatively instrumental perspective of 'providing business opportunities'.

A partner state would respond to the emergence of non-profit-seeking economic practices at least as actively and positively as it does to the commercial entities of the platform economy. This would imply breaking away from the narrow understandings of 'economic activity' (as something indicated by the GDP) and 'employment' (as either wage labour or high-growth entrepreneurship) in order to build the understanding about how the self-organised economies in tandem and in a strategic coordination with the welfare state policies could contribute to the overall well-being and sustainability of a society (see Chapters 1 and 3). As Ann Light and Clodaugh Miskelly (2015) argue, the sharing economy is after all not so much about 'the economy' in the sense of making profit, but about enabling co-operation in a variety of new cultural forms

A partner state could support self-organised ridesharing both through 'positive' and 'negative' routes. 'Negative' support would imply a deliberate choice to prevent overregulation (the 'Inaction' path in Chapter 1), since it easily damages self-organised economic communities by interpreting them as conventional economic actors and by imposing requirements that were crafted with a completely different context in mind. A more *positive* approach would imply recognising how various forms of the sharing economy promote social well-being and ecological sustainability and providing incentives that actually encourage the expanding the scope of such activities (the 'Creating background conditions' path in Chapter 1). Naturally, taking one or both of these routes would require a deeper understanding of the different forms and functions of 'sharing' (Schor 2014; Martin 2016; Kennedy 2016), articulating the need to draw boundaries between the ones that should be *supported*, the ones that should be *opposed*, and the ones that are *neutral* or *ambivalent* in their likely social and ecological outcomes.

Ridesharing has the potential to upscale old practices of *ad hoc* mutual aid to a level where they might have significant impacts in reorganising transport and reducing its carbon footprint. This extent of upscaling, and especially the wish that ridesharing would attract new users from car drivers instead of public transport passengers, is unlikely to occur spontaneously but would require government intervention to discourage the habit of driving alone. An example of incentivising ridesharing would be a taxation scheme where driving a car would be taxed with a different per kilometre price depending on the rate of occupancy: ridesharing would then provide the possibility to share not only the direct expenses of driving (the cost of electricity or gasoline) but also its emissions footprint expressed in the driving tax. Without strategic intervention, and without a more conscious objective setting from within the ridesharing community itself, the more probable path is that self-organised ridesharing becomes challenged or even outcompeted by commercial mobility-as-a-service operators.

7

Epilogue: On the possibilities to learn from the Global South

Laura Kumpuniemi & Sanna Ryynänen

The articles in this book have theorised different types of community economies and their relations to the Nordic welfare state. One of the cross-cutting themes has related to the need for redefinitions and reconceptualisations of concepts such as wellbeing, value, employment and economic activity, as they are approached from the perspective of community economies instead of the prevailing model of the welfare state. Moreover, the need to develop the existing system and the informative role of community economies in this development has been highlighted.

In this short commentary, we turn our attention towards southern societal contexts in order to ask what could northern community economies learn from the rich traditions and experiences of alternative economies in the Global South. Due to the focus of our research and other related activities, we concentrate on the experiences in South America, and more specifically, in Bolivia and Brazil. Our notions should therefore be taken as exemplifying rather than anything covering the heterogeneity of the Global South. Also, we do not aim to present ourselves here as 'voices from the South' but to recognise our position as northern researchers learning from and with the South.

Different contexts create different alternatives

For the sake of contextualisation, the specificity of the Nordic welfare state model and its key differences with the South (American) context should be noted. These different social and economic contexts in the South and North also have an impact in what type of community economy and self-organised economic activities are encouraged. To start with, the sense of security or vulnerability differ rather drastically between North and South. The central idea of the Nordic welfare state is to secure social assistance in order to prevent full exclusion of vulnerable people, such as the sick or unemployed. In the Global South, in most cases the state is not the key player safeguarding people, which leads to the necessity of relying on personal social networks for care and safety. Working conditions further contribute to this precarity, as the working population is often employed in self-created informal sector jobs and has to rely on several sources of income. Moreover, the notion of trust differentiates rather remarkably the northern and southern contexts. In the Nordic welfare states, the level of trust towards other people and the government is the highest in the world with over 60 percent of the population trusting other people, whereas in the Global South the level of trust tends to be notoriously low. This is further highlighted in countries like Brazil, Ecuador and Peru, where less than 10 percent of the population express trust towards other people. (Inglehart et al. 2014.)

This superficial comparison suffices to make the point that the function of community economies is potentially rather different in these different contexts. In the North, the activists of community economies might enjoy relatively good economic support either in the form of employment or benefits, and choices to turn to alternative economies might be more pronouncedly ideological. In the Global South, reducing vulnerability through offering possibilities for employment is often highlighted as the key role of alternative economies. Community economies and solidarity initiatives are often seen as a way to fill in the gaps in official social security systems (Hillenkamp et al. 2013). However, these activities have other dimensions. These alternative means of subsistence follow a different logic than that of the capitalist economy, and they put this logic concretely into action through practices of reciprocity and cooperation (Carneiro 2011, 85–86). When economic activity is directed to community and cooperation rather than to individual gains and competition, it offers valuable spaces for building trust, among other things. Community economy initiatives can also be instrumental in building capabilities for cooperation, as well as to strengthen social networks in order to create democratic processes within communities. Sometimes they also enhance possibilities for local political control by encouraging and advocating for workers' participation in local decision-making. (Hillenkamp et al. 2013, 12.) Especially the solidarity economy, a prominent strand of community economies in Latin America, offers a newly politicised perspective for approaching the mainstream economy while securing livelihoods for many through its various forms. Ethan Miller (2004) describes solidarity economy as a form of economic organising that can reinforce new kinds of economic relations in communities and build spaces based on non-capitalist values like solidarity, democratisation, cooperation, and mutual support. It is essentially not an economic model but rather supports the idea of recognising diverse practices and respecting difference. Awareness of existing practices also helps to expand the ways that economy is understood and to realise that economic practices outside of capitalism already exist. (Miller 2004.)

Intermediating layers and pedagogies
In Brazil, the manifestation of the solidarity economy can be portrayed as being comprised of three different 'layers', forming an architecture of a country-wide movement that stretches from local activists to government initiatives. As such, it presents a different model of organising alternative economy than the more or less self-organised community economy initiatives presented

in this volume. Firstly, there is a grassroots level of community economy initiatives and enterprises, that is, collectives based on self-management and cooperation (cooperatives, exchange circles, associations, etc.) aimed at production of goods, service provision, recycling, finance, solidarity consumption, etc. The number of identified solidarity economy initiatives in 2013 was over 30 000 (SIES 2013). Secondly, there are different types of civil support entities, such as university 'incubators', NGOs, trade unions, and microfinanciers that aim at encouraging as well as channelling solidarity economy needs by offering training, research, advisory, microcredits, and legal consultancy. Third, there are policy-makers and local as well as national public policies that aim at formulation, coordination, and implementation of solidarity economy policies and initiation of public funding programmes. One example at the public policy level was the National Secretary of Solidarity Economy (SENAES) that was established within the Brazilian Ministry of Labour in 2002, during the government of president Lula. However, it should be noted that SENAES was considerably downgraded during the government of the former president Michel Temer in 2016 and abolished in its initial form by the government of the current president Jair Bolsonaro in January 2019.

When attention is directed towards possibilities to learn from and within Brazilian experiences, the second 'layer' of so-called civil support entities is of specific interest. In Brazil, the solidarity economy is often seen not only as a question of economic organizing but also of pedagogics (e.g. Gadotti 2009; Jaramillo and Carreon 2014). From this perspective, solidarity economy is not only a way of organising economic activities, but also a process of collaborative learning and problem-solving, rooted in concrete life situations. The pedagogical nature of the solidarity economy also implies that the concept and the related values are systematically promoted. One concrete example of this are the solidarity economy incubators found in more than one hundred Brazilian public universities. The incubators are one example of the so-called university extension practices, where universities work in close collaboration with the surrounding communities. In regard to solidarity economy incubators, this means promoting the solidarity economy through action research processes where all involved parties both learn and pass on their own accumulated knowledge, be it academic or practical.

The pedagogical institutional support of the conditions for the solidarity economy creates an increasing amount of knowledge on the solidarity economy and its practices. Yet it should also be understood as a promotion of practices that aim to appreciate the value and dignity of all people, reinforcing solidarity, and increasing cooperation and reciprocity. (See Gadotti 2009; Lopes et al. 2005.) This is something that should be taken into account in the North as well.

Another story of 'the partner state'
Both in Brazil and Bolivia, the state and other public entities have (had) an important role in supporting community economies. This kind of model exemplifies one type of 'partner state' (see Chapter 6) where the state has provided incentives for expanding the scope of community economy activities. However, whereas the welfare state model poses the question of disciplining authorities in relation to the community economies (Chapter 3), the model that leans more towards a 'partner state' has raised questions about control as well as processes of domestication. For instance, the idea of a plural economy that includes the notion of community-focused economic practices, which is something that the Bolivian government during president Evo Morales' era (2006-19) embraced, was a disappointment. Although legislation now recognizes community and solidarity economy, the implementation of the laws is non-existent and the government's focus has been more in the state-led economy and an increase

in extractivist economy. Meanwhile, the initiatives promoting community economy have become more fragmented and more dependent on the government. (Wanderley et al. 2015.) Moreover, the plural economy agenda has not been put into practice hand in hand with fundamental plans for democratisation, so the anti-democratic tendencies in Bolivia have also undermined the progressive intentions to change the basis for economy and wellbeing.

In Bolivia, there have been attempts to apply the idea of alternative economic models through the notion of *vivir bien* and placing emphasis on the values of the Mother Earth at the state level. The concept of *vivir bien* is based on the Ecuadorian and Bolivian indigenous people's concept of good life, emphasising harmony with nature and other people. It is also presented as an alternative to capitalist development and commodification and, thereby, as an example of decolonial efforts. (Gudynas 2011.) However, *vivir bien* has not changed governmental practices as radically as was hoped. Neoliberal practices at the state level have been continued, and although institutionalisation of social movements has enhanced their participation in decision-making processes, it has also resulted in disciplining and controlling them. (Ranta 2014, 222.) In Brazil during the government of the Workers' Party, there were policy programmes supporting solidarity economy actors, but no law on solidarity economy was passed (Esteves 2014, 85). Also, the politics of the Brazil's current right-wing president Jair Bolsonaro do not portray a very promising future for the rather radical interpretations of solidarity economy that characterised the work of the National Secretary of Solidarity Economy.

The experiences from Bolivia and Brazil can be used for learning purposes to see what kind of developments follow the attempts of upscaling community economies to the state level. They show that the notion of the partner state might also be a problematic approach to the building of community economies. Coraggio

(2011, 44) suggests that the state as a structure should be overcome altogether because the representative system leads to promoting the interests of central economic groups making the unjust and socially inefficient system governable. Community economies, and solidarity economy especially, advocate for democratisation that could rather refer to the enforcing of local communities and the grassroots level self-organisation independent from the state, that is, participatory democracy instead of representative one. According to Ana Margarida Esteves (2014, 76), not only policies and regulation are needed for ensuring the expansion of non-capitalist production, commercialisation and finance, but also strong structures that guarantee a process of thorough democratisation by distributing power and ensuring direct participation.

The partner state discussed by Venäläinen (Chapter 6) and Eskelinen (Chapter 2) in this book has, therefore, to be thought of with care, as state involvement might take away a lot of the self-organising elements of grassroots actors. It could also make the structures that were originally thriving for non-hierarchical models rather hierarchical in the end, and even allow them to be hijacked by bureaucracy, as for example has been the case in Bolivia. However, the partner state idea can be seen in a quite different light in different parts of the world, as there are differences between the political stability in the South and the North. There have been changes towards more instability in the North, but nevertheless the politics have tended to be more unstable in the South where there can be a regime change that diverts the politics almost overnight into a totally opposite direction. Although there are signs of changes, policy-formation in welfare states in the long term has taken place through a moderately strong consensus between political parties, which has secured a decent level of political stability.

Conclusions

All in all, in the South there are experiences, knowledges and ongoing processes in the area of community economy building that actors in the North should take notice of if there are aspirations to develop a more comprehensive community economy practice and a movement. The examples in this book show that there are already many existing practices that follow a rationale differing from the capitalist logic. The strengthening of community-based alternatives needs to be based on processes that count on learning and reciprocity on local and global levels. The practices are not directly applicable from one context to another, but where there is a common value base and similar ambitions, there is great opportunity for cross-continent learning. This does also not mean idealising the experiences of the South but rather the relationships between the North and the South in this sense should be directed to learning from both successes and failures.

One concrete example of learning possibilities are the solidarity economy incubators in Brazil and the active role the universities have taken in promoting the solidarity economy. In addition to the incubators, some of the universities have constructed counter-hegemonic economic understanding by providing courses on solidarity and community economies. When the economic and environmental crises intertwine into a destructive spiral, 'it is useless to use all our energies in verbal attacks against capitalism,' as Gadotti (2009, 123) states. Alternatives should not only be made at the grassroots level, but also actively promoted. One possibility for that could be universities and other educational institutions in the North taking inspiration from the Brazilian incubators in order to encourage the growth of community economies.

7 – On the possibilities to learn from the Global South

Bibliography

Alber, J. and Kohler, U. 2008. 'Informal Food Production in the Enlarged European Union.' *Social Indicators Research Journal* 89, 113–127.

Alexander, S. 2015. 'Basic and maximum income.' In D'Alisa, G., Demaria, F. and Kallis, G. (eds.) *Degrowth. A Vocabulary for a new Era.* New York and London: Routledge, 146–149.

Arendt, H. (1958) 2013. *The Human Condition.* Chicago: University of Chicago Press.

Arvidsson, A. and Peitersen, N. 2016. *The Ethical Economy. Rebuilding Value After the Crisis.* New York: Columbia University Press.

Autio, M., Collins, R., Wahlen, S. and Anttila, M. 2013. 'Consuming nostalgia? The appreciation of authenticity in local food production.' *International Journal of Consumer Studies* 37(5), 564–568.

Autotalli.com. 2018. 'Vaihtoautolistaus.' [A listing of second-hand cars.] Models from 2006(n=1545). https://www.autotalli.com/vaihtoautot/listaa/vuosimalli_min/2006/vuosimalli_max/2006/sivu/39 (accessed 8 December 2018).

Bailey, D. 2015. 'The environmental paradox of the welfare state: The dynamics of sustainability.' *New Political Economy* 20(6), 793–811.

Bauwens, M. 2012. 'Blueprint for P2P society: The partner state & ethical economy.' https://www.shareable.net/blog/blueprint-for-p2p-society-the-partner-state-ethical-economy (accessed 11 November 2018).

Bauwens, M. and Ramos, J. 2018. 'Re-imagining the left through an ecology of the commons: towards a post-capitalist commons transition.' *Global Discourse* 8(2), 325–342.

Bauwens, M., and Kostakis, V. 2014. *Network Society and Future Scenarios for a Collaborative Economy.* Basingstoke: Palgrave MacMillan.

Benkler, Yochai. 2004. 'Sharing nicely: On shareable goods and the emergence of sharing as a modality of economic production.' *Yale Law Journal* 114(2), 273–358.

Blay-Palmer, A. (ed.). 2010. *Imagining Sustainable Food Systems: Theory and*

Bibliography

Practice. London and New York: Routledge.

Boje, T. P. and Leira, A. (eds.). 2000. *Gender, Welfare State and the Market: Towards a New Division of Labour*. London: Routlegde.

Bollier, D. 2011. 'The commons, short and sweet.' http://bollier.org/commons-short-and-sweet (accessed 28 January 2013).

Boyle, D. and Bird, S. 2014. *Give and Take. How Timebanking is Transforming Healthcare*. Stroud: Timebanking UK.

Boyle, D. and Harris, M. 2009. *The Challenge of Co-Production*. London: NESTA / New Economics Foundation.

Boyle, D., Slay, J. and Stephens, L. 2010. *Public Services Inside Out. Putting Co-Production into Practice*. London: NESTA / New Economics Foundation.

Bradshaw, C. 2018. 'Waste law and the value of food.' *Journal of Environmental Law* 30(2), 311–332.

Bruns, A. 2007. 'Produsage: Towards a broader framework for user-led content creation.' In *Creativity and Cognition: Proceedings of the 6th ACM SIGCHI Conference on Creativity & Cognition*, Washington, DC: ACM.

Buch-Hansen, H. 2018. 'The prerequisites for a degrowth paradigm shift: Insights from critical political economy.' *Ecological Economics* 146, 157–163.

Burawoy, M. 1989. 'The extended case method.' *Sociological Theory* 16(1), 4–33.

Buttel, F.H. 2003. 'Internalizing the societal costs of agricultural production.' *Plant Physiology* 133(4), 1656–1665.

Cahn, E. S. 2004. *No More Throw-Away People: The Co-Production Imperative*. Washington, DC: Essential Books.

Cahn, E. S. 2009. 'It's the core economy stupid: An open letter to the non-profit community.' https://timebanks.org/wp-content/uploads/2014/01/CoreEconomyOp-Ed_001.pdf (accessed 11 June 2019).

Callon, M. 1998. 'Introduction.' In Callon, M. (ed.). *The Laws of the Markets*. Malden: Blackwell, 1–57.

Calvo-Porral, C., Faina, A. and Lopez, C.H. 2016. 'Can marketing help in tackling food waste? Proposals in developed countries.' *Journal of Food Products Marketing* 23(1), 42–60.

Cameron, J. and Gordon, R. 2010. 'Building sustainable and ethical food futures through economic diversity: Options for a mid-sized city.' Paper presented at the *Policy Workshop on The Future of Australia's Mid-Sized Cities,* Latrobe University, Bendigo, VIC, 28 and 29 Sept.

Carneiro, V. 2011. 'Entre o público e o privado: uma reflexão sobre o lugar da ação política na prática da economia solidária no Brasil.' [Between the public and the private: a reflection about the place of political action in the practice of solidarity economy in Brazil.] In P. Hespanha and A. Mendonça dos Santos (eds.). *Economia Solidária: Questões Teóricas e Epistemológicas.* [Solidarity economy: Theoretical and epistemological questions.] Série políticas sociais. Coimbra, Portugal: CES and Almedina, 83–111.

Chambon, N. 2011. *Food program under discussion: the end of a European solidarity towards the most deprived persons? Understanding the ongoing debate.* Extract of the policy paper N°45 « Is the CAP a ground for European solidarity or disunion? Notre Europe June 2011. https://institutdelors.eu/wp-content/uploads/2018/01/extracts-en.pdf (accessed 11 June 2019).

Chan, N. D., and Shaheen, S. A. 2012. 'Ridesharing in North America: Past, present, and future.' *Transport Reviews 32*(1), 93–112.

Community Economies. 2019. 'Key ideas. Community economies.' http://www.communityeconomies.org/key-ideas (accessed 15 March 2019).

Coote, A. 2010. *The Great Transition: Social Justice and the Core Economy.* London: New Economics Foundation.

Coote, A. 2011. 'Big society and the new austerity.' In M. Stott (ed.). *The Big Society Challenge.* Cardiff: Keystone Development Trust, 82–94.

Coote, A. 2013. 'Introduction: A new economics of work and time.' In Coote, A. and Franklin, J. (eds.). *Time on Our Side: Why We All Need a Shorter Working Week.* London: New Economics Foundation, ix–xxii.

Coote, A. and Franklin, J. (eds.). 2013. *Time on Our Side: Why We All Need a Shorter Working Week.* London: New Economics Foundation.

Coraggio, J. L. 2011. *Economía social y solidaria. El trabajo antes que el capital.* [Social and solidarity economy. Work before capital.] Acosta, A. and Martínez, E. (eds.). Quito: Abya Yala.

Cowan, M. 2015. 'BlaBlaCar has turned ride-sharing into a multi-million-euro business.' *Wired UK.* https://www.wired.co.uk/article/blablacar (accessed 11

Bibliography

June 2019).

D'Alisa, G., Demaria, F. and Kallis, G. (eds.). 2015. *Degrowth: A Vocabulary for a New Era*. New York & London: Routledge.

De Angelis, M. 2007. *The Beginning of History: Value Struggles and Global Capital*. London: Pluto Press.

De Angelis, M. 2013. 'Does capital need a commons fix?' *Ephemera: Theory & Politics in Organization* 13(3), 603–615.

De Angelis, M. 2017. *Omnia Sunt Communia*. London: Zed Books.

De Armiño, K.P. 2014. 'Erosion of rights, uncritical solidarity and food banks in Spain.' In T. Silvasti and G. Riches (eds.). *First World Hunger Revisited. Food Charity or the Right to Food?* London: Palgrave Macmillan, 131–145.

Development Initiatives. 2017. *Global Nutrition Report 2017: Nourishing the SDGs*. Bristol: Development Initiatives.

Dittrich M., Giljum S., Lutter S. and Polzin C. 2012. *Green Economies Around the World? Implications of Resource Use for Development and the Environment*. Wien: Sustainable Europe Research Institute.

Domene, J. F. 2012. 'Calling and career outcome expectations: The mediating role of self-efficacy.' *Journal of Career Assessment*, 20(3), 281–292.

Dowler, E. 2014. 'Food banks and food justice in "austerity Britain".' In T. Silvasti and G. Riches (eds.). *First World Hunger Revisited. Food Charity or the Right to Food*. London: Palgrave Macmillan, 160–175.

Eisler, R. 2007. *The Real Wealth of Nations: Creating a Caring Economics*. San Francisco: Brett-Koehler Publishers.

Ellison, N. 2005. *The Transformation of Welfare States?* London and New York: Routledge.

Eskelinen, T. 2018. 'Social space for self-organising. An exploratory study of timebanks in Finland and in the UK.' *Nordic Journal of Social Research* 9(1), 89–109.

Eskelinen, T., and Venäläinen, J. forthcoming. 'Unveiling the "social excess of exchange" in self-organized alternative economies.'

Eskelinen, T., Kovanen, S. and van der Wekken, R. 2017. 'Self-organisation in solidarity economies.' *The Finnish Journal of Urban Studies* 55(3). http://www.yss.fi/journal/self-organisation-in-solidarity-economies/

Esping-Andersen, G. 1990. *The Three Worlds of Welfare Capitalism*. Cambridge: Polity Press.

Esteves, A. M. 2014. 'Decolonizing livelihoods, decolonizing the will: Solidarity economy as a social justice paradigm in Latin America.' In Michael Reisch (ed.). *Routledge International Handbook of Social Justice*. Abingdon: Routledge, 74–90.

European Community. 1986. 'Food surpluses: Disposal for welfare purposes.' *Agricultural Information Services* 2/1986.

European CSA Research Group. 2016. *Overview of Community Supported Agriculture in Europe*. Urgenci: The International Network for Community Supported Agriculture.

EEA [European Environmental Agency]. 2018. *Perspectives on Transitions to Sustainability*. EEA Report No 25/2017. Denmark: EEA.

European Social Fund Plus. 2018. 'EU budget: A new social Fund and globalisation adjustment fund. https://ec.europa.eu/social/main.jsp?catId=89&furtherNews=yes&newsId=9114&langId=en (accessed 11 June 2019).

Evans, A. and Nagele, R. 2018. 'A lot to digest: Advancing food waste policy in the United States.' *Natural Resources Journal* 58(7). http://digitalrepository.unm.edu/nrj/vol58/iss1/7

Evira. 2017. 'Ruoka-apuun luovutettavat elintarvikkeet.' [Foodstuff delivered for food aid.] Instruction of the Finnish Food Authority Evira, 16035/2.

FBA [Finnish Beekeepers' Association]. 2015. *Mehiläishoitajien määrän kasvu jatkuu* [Increase in the number of beekeepers continues]. 8 January 2015. https://www.mehilaishoitajat.fi/?x118281=1896343 (accessed 18 December 2018).

FAO. 2011. *Global Food Losses and Food Waste. Extent, Causes and Prevention: Study conducted for the International Congress SAVE FOOD! at Interpack2011 Düsseldorf, Germany*. Rome: Food and Agriculture Organization of the United Nations. http://www.fao.org/docrep/014/mb060e/mb060e00.pdf (accessed 11 June 2019).

FAO. 2014. *The State of Food and Agriculture. Innovation in family farming*. Rome: FAO.

Bibliography

FAO, IFAD, UNICEF, WFP and WHO. 2018. *The State of Food Security and Nutrition in the World 2018. Building climate resilience for food security and nutrition.* Rome: FAO.

Farrants, K. and Bambra, C. 2018. 'Neoliberalism and the recommodification of health inequalities: A case study of the Swedish welfare state 1980 to 2011.' *Scandinavian Journal of Public Health* 46(1), 18–26.

FICoAS [Finnish Information Centre of Automobile Sector]. 2018a. 'Ajoneuvokannan kehitys.' [The development of the numbers of cars.] Updated January 29, 2018. http://www.aut.fi/tilastot/autokannan_kehitys/ajoneuvokannan_kehitys (accessed 8 December 2018).

FICoAS. 2018b. 'Autokannan keski-iän kehitys.' [The development of the average age of cars.] Updated January 18, 2018. http://www.aut.fi/tilastot/autokannan_kehitys/autokannan_keski-ian_kehitys (accessed 8 December 2018).

Finnish Forest Research Institute (2012) 'Recreational use of forests. Outdoor recreational statistics 2010.' Updated 28th February 2012. http://www.metla.fi/metinfo/monikaytto/lvvi/en/statistics_2010/2010-table13.htm (accessed 30 Novermber 2018).

Fitzpatrick, T. 2011. 'Environmental justice: philosophies and practices.' In Fitzpatrick, T. (ed.) *Understanding the Environment and Social Policy.* Bristol: Policy Press, 131–154.

Fitzpatrick, T. and Cahill, M. 2002. 'The new environment of welfare.' In Fitzpatrick, T. and Cahill, M. (eds.) *Environment and Welfare: Towards a Green Social Policy.* Basingstoke: Palgrave Macmillan, 1–20.

Folke, C., Biggs, R., Norstrom, A. V., Reyers, B., AND Rockstrom, J. 2016. 'Social-ecological resilience and biosphere-based sustainability science.' *Ecology and Society* 21(3), 41.

Forssell, S. 2017. *Perspectives on the Sustainability Promise of Alternative Food Networks.* PhD Thesis. Helsinki: University of Helsinki, Department of Economics and Management.

Franklin, A. 1999. *Animals and Modern Cultures. A Sociology of Human-Animal Relations in Modernity.* London: Sage.

FTA [Finnish Transport Agency]. 2017. 'Tieverkko.' [The road network.] Updated March 6, 2017. https://vayla.fi/tieverkko#.XOT-HMgzaUk (accessed 8 December 2018).

FTA 2018. 'Liikenneviraston tilinpäätös 2017.' [The financial statement of Finnish Transport Agency for 2017.] https://julkaisut.liikennevirasto.fi/pdf8/lr_2018_liikenneviraston_tilinpaatos_2017_web.pdf (accessed 8 December 2018).

Fuchs, C. 2012. 'Dallas Smythe today – The audience commodity, the digital labour debate, Marxist political economy and critical theory. Prolegomena to a digital labour theory of value.' *TripleC: Communication, Capitalism & Critique. Open Access Journal for a Global Sustainable Information Society* 10(2), 692–740.

Gadotti, M. 2009. *Economia solidária como práxis pedagógica*. [Solidarity economy as pedagogic practice.] São Paulo: Editora e Livraria Instituto Paulo Freire.

Gibson-Graham, J.K. 2006a. *The End of Capitalism (as we knew it). A Feminist Critique of Political Economy*. Minneapolis: University of Minnesota Press.

Gibson-Graham, J.K. 2006b. *A Postcapitalist Politics*. Minneapolis: University of Minnesota Press.

Gibson-Graham, J.K. 2008. 'Diverse economies: Performative practices for other worlds.' *Progress in Human Geography*, 32(5), 613–632.

Gibson-Graham, J.K. and Community Economies Collective. 2017. 'Cultivating community economies. Tools for building a liveable world.' *The Next System Project*. https://thenextsystem.org/cultivating-community-economies (accessed 3 March 2018)

Gibson-Graham, J.K. and Roelvink, G. 2011. 'The nitty gritty of creating alternative economies.' *Social Alternatives* 30(1), 29–33.

González, S. J. 2013. 'Abstract labour theory of value and theory of price.' IDEAS Working Paper Series from RePEc. https://ideas.repec.org/p/col/000089/010735.html

Gough, I. 2017. *Heat, Greed and Human Need: Climate Change, Capitalism and Sustainable Wellbeing*. Cheltenham: Edward Elgar Publishing.

Graeber, D. 2013. 'It is value that brings universes into being.' *HAU: Journal of Ethnographic Theory* 3(2), 219–243.

Graeber, David. 2014. 'On the moral grounds of economic relations: A Maussian approach.' *Journal of Classical Sociology* 14(1), 65–77. https://doi.

Bibliography

org/10.1177/1468795X13494719.

Graeber, D. 2018. *Bullshit Jobs: A Theory.* New York: Simon & Schuster.

Gregory, L. 2015. *Trading Time: Can Exchange Lead to Social Change?* Bristol: Policy Press.

Gritzas, G. and Kavoulakos, K. I. 2016. 'Diverse economies and alternative spaces: An overview of approaches and practices.' *European Urban and Regional Studies.* 23(4), 917–934.

Gudynas, E. 2011. 'Buen vivir: Today's tomorrow.' *Development* 54(4), 441–447.

Günther, F. 2001. 'Fossil energy and food security.' *Energy & Environment* 12(4), 253–273.

Hagfors, R., Kajanoja, J. and Komu, M. 2014. 'The virtuous circle of the welfare state revisited.' Kela working papers 54. Helsinki: Kela Research Department

Hagolani-Albov, S. E. 2017. 'Urban agriculture in Helsinki, Finland.' *Focus on Geography* 1/2017.

Halpern, D. 2010. *The Hidden Wealth of Nations.* Cambridge: Polity Press.

Hamari, J., Sjöklint, M., and Ukkonen, A. 2015. 'The sharing economy: Why people participate in collaborative consumption.' *Journal of the Association for Information Science and Technology* 67(9), 2047–2059.

Haraway, D. 1988. 'Situated knowledges: The science question in feminism and the privilege of partial perspective.' *Feminist Studies* 14(3), 575–599.

Haraway, D. 2008. *When Species Meet.* Minneapolis: University of Minnesota Press.

Haraway, D. 2016. *Staying with the Trouble: Making Kin in the Chthulucene.* Durham: Duke University Press.

Harris, E. 2009. 'Neoliberal subjectivities or a politics of the possible? Reading for difference in alternative food networks.' *Area* 41(1), 55–63.

HE 309/1993 vp. 'Hallituksen esitys eduskunnalle perustuslakien perusoikeussäännösten muuttamisesta.' [Government proposal to the Parliament on the amend the Fundamental Rights Regulation of the Constitution]. https://www.eduskunta.fi/FI/vaski/sivut/trip.aspx?triptype=ValtiopaivaAsiat&docid=he+309/1993 (accessed 11 June 2019)

Healy, S. 2009. 'Alternative economies.' In R. Kitchin and N. Thrift (eds.).

International Encyclopedia of Human Geography. Amsterdam: Elsevier, 338–344.

Hearn, A. 2010. 'Structuring feeling: Web 2.0, online ranking and rating, and the digital "reputation" economy.' *Ephemera: Theory & Politics in Organization* 10(3–4), 421–438.

Helfrich, S. 2013. 'Economics and commons?! Towards a commons-creating peer economy.' In *Economics and the Common(s): From Seed Form to Core Paradigm. A Report on an International Conference on the Future of the Commons*. Berlin: Heinrich Böll Foundation. https://www.boell.de/sites/default/files/ecc_report_final.pdf

Helsingin Uutiset. 2010. 'Kimppakyytien välitys netissä yleistyy rajusti.' [Online ridematching is growing rapidly]. *Helsingin Uutiset* 16. November 2010. https://www.helsinginuutiset.fi/artikkeli/4725-kimppakyytien-valitys-netissa-yleistyy-rajusti (accessed 13 June 2019).

Henderson, T. 2017. 'Real freedom for all revisited – Normative justifications of basic income.' *Basic Income Studies* 12(1), 242–276.

Hillenkamp, I., Lapeyre, F. and Lemaître, A. 2013. 'Solidarity economy as a part of popular security enhancing practices. A neo-Polanyian conceptual framework.' UNRISD Conference Papers.

Hirvilammi, T. and Helne, T. 2014. 'Changing paradigms: A sketch for sustainable wellbeing and ecosocial policy.' *Sustainability* 6(4), 2160–2175.

Hochschild, A. R. 1989. *The Second Shift: Working Parents and the Revolution at Home*. New York: Viking.

Hoegh-Guldberg, O., Jacob, D., Taylor, M., Bindi, M., Brown, S., Camilloni, I., Diedhiou, A., Djalante, R., Ebi, K., Engelbrecht, F., Guiot, J., Hijioka, Y., Mehrotra, S., Payne, A., Seneviratne, S. I., Thomas, A., Warren, R., Zhou G. 2018. 'Impacts of 1.5°C Global Warming on Natural and Human Systems.' In V. Masson-Delmotte, P. Zhai, H. O. Pörtner, D. Roberts, J. Skea, P.R. Shukla, A. Pirani, W. Moufouma-Okia, C. Péan, R. Pidcock, S. Connors, J. B. R. Matthews, Y. Chen, X. Zhou, M. I. Gomis, E. Lonnoy, T. Maycock, M. Tignor, T. Waterfield (eds.). *Global warming of 1.5°C. An IPCC Special Report on the impacts of global warming of 1.5°C above pre-industrial levels and related global greenhouse gas emission pathways, in the context of strengthening the global response to the threat of climate change, sustainable*

Bibliography

development, and efforts to eradicate poverty. Switzerland: IPCC.

Houtbeckers, E. 2018. 'Framing social enterprise as post-growth organising in the diverse economy.' *Management Revue* 29(3), 257–280.

Hyvärinen, P. 2017. 'Ruoantuotannon ristiriitoja rikkaruohonjuuritasolla. Kitkeminen työnä, tiedontuotantona ja tulevaisuuksien tekemisenä.' [Grassroots level complexities. Weeding as work, knowledge production and enacting the future]. *Sukupuolentutkimus-Genusforskning* 30(2), 35–48.

Ingham, G. 2004. *The Nature of Money.* Cambridge: Polity Press.

Inglehart, R., Haerpfer, C., Moreno, A., Welzel, C., Kizilova, K., Diez-Medrano, J., Lagos, M., Norris, P., Ponarin, E. and Puranen, B. et al. (eds.). 2014. *World Values Survey: Round Six - Country-Pooled Datafile Version.* Madrid: JD Systems Institute. www.worldvaluessurvey.org/WVSDocumentationWV6.jsp

IPCC. 2018. *Global warming of 1.5°C. An IPCC Special Report on the impacts of global warming of 1.5°C above pre-industrial levels and related global greenhouse gas emission pathways, in the context of strengthening the global response to the threat of climate change, sustainable development, and efforts to eradicate poverty* [V. Masson-Delmotte, P. Zhai, H. O. Pörtner, D. Roberts, J. Skea, P.R. Shukla, A. Pirani, W. Moufouma-Okia, C. Péan, R. Pidcock, S. Connors, J. B. R. Matthews, Y. Chen, X. Zhou, M. I. Gomis, E. Lonnoy, T. Maycock, M. Tignor, T. Waterfield (eds.)].

Iqbal, R. and Todi, P. 2015. 'The Nordic model: Existence, emergence and sustainability.' *Procedia Economics and Finance* 30, 336–351.

Ironmonger, D. 1996. 'Counting outputs, capital inputs and caring labor: Estimating gross household product.' *Feminist Economics* 2(3), 37–64.

Jackson, T. 2013. 'The trouble with productivity.' In Coote, A. and Franklin, J. (eds.). *Time on Our Side: Why We All Need a Shorter Working Week.* London: New Economics Foundation, 25–30.

Jaramillo, N.E. and Carreon, M.E. 2014. 'Pedagogies of resistance and solidarity: towards revolutionary and decolonial praxis.' *Interface: A Journal for and about Social Movements* 6(1), 392–411.

Jehlicka, P., Kostelecký, T. and Smith, J. 2013. 'Food self-provisioning in Czechia: Beyond coping strategy of the poor: A response to Alber and Kohler's "Informal food production in the enlarged European Union" (2008).' *Social Indicators Research*, 111(1), 219–234.

Johansson, H. 2001. 'Activation Policies in the Nordic Countries: Social Democratic Universalism under Pressure.' *Journal of European Area Studies* 9(1), 63–77.

John, N. A. 2017. *The Age of Sharing*. London: Polity Press.

Johnston, A., Kornelakis, A. and d'Acri, C. R. 2011. 'Social partners and the welfare state: Recalibration, privatization or collectivization of social risks?.' *European Journal of Industrial Relations* 17(4), 349–364.

Jonas, A. E. G. 2013. 'Place and region III: Alternative regionalisms.' *Progress in Human Geography* 37(6), 822–828.

Joutsenvirta, M. 2016. 'A practice approach to the institutionalization of economic degrowth.' *Ecological Economics* 128, 23–32.

Kallis, G. 2018. *Degrowth*. Newcastle Upon Tyne: Agenda Publishing.

Kallis, G., Kerschner, C. and Martinez-Alier, J. 2012. 'The economics of degrowth.' *Ecological Economics* 84, 172–180.

Kennedy, J. 2016. 'Conceptual boundaries of sharing.' *Information, Communication & Society* 19(4), 461–474.

Kildal, N. and Kuhnle, S. 2005. *Normative Foundations of the Welfare State: The Nordic Experience*. London: Routledge.

Kleijn, D., Winfree, R., Bartomeus, I., Carvalheiro, L. G., Henry, M., Isaacs, R., Klein, A., Kremen, C., M'Gonigle, L.K., Rader, R., Ricketts, T.H., Williams, N.M., Adamson, N.L., Ascher, J.S., Báldi, A., Batáry, P., Benjamin, F., Biesmeijer, J.C., Blitzer, E.J., Bommarco, R., Brand, M. R.,Bretagnolle, V., Button, L., Cariveau, D.P., Chifflet, R., Colville, J.F., Danforth, B.N., Elle, E., Garratt, M.P.D., Herzog, F., Holzschuh, A., Howlett, B.G., Jauker, F., Jha, S., Knop, E., Krewenka, K.M., Le Féon, V., Mandelik, Y., May, E.A., Park, M.G., Pisanty, G., Reemer, M., Riedinger, V., Rollin, O., Rundlöf, M., Sardiñas, H.S., Scheper, J., Sciligo, A.R., Smith, H.G., Steffan-Dewenter, I., Thorp, R., Tscharntke, T., Verhulst, J., Viana, B.F., Vaissière, B.E., Veldtman, R., Westphal, C. and Potts, S.G. (2015) 'Delivery of crop pollination services is an insufficient argument for wild pollinator conservation.' *Nature Communications* 6, article number 7414.

Kloo, D. E. 2015. 'The sustainability of welfare capitalism. Redefining institutions and agency.' In Borgnäs, K., Eskelinen, T., Perkiö, J. and

Bibliography

Warlenius, R. (eds.). *The Politics of Ecosocialism: Transforming Welfare*. London and New York: Routledge, 34–52.

Knuuttila, M. and Vatanen, E. 2015. *Elintarvikemarkkinoiden tuontiriippuvuus* [Dependency of Food Production and Markets on Imported Food and Inputs]. Helsinki: Luonnonvarakeskus.

Koch, M., and Mont, O. (eds.). 2016. *Sustainability and the Political Economy of Welfare*. London and New York: Routledge.

Koivusilta, L., Vaarno, J., Marttunen, K., Hynynen, A., Nieminen, T., Niemi, J. K., Harjunpää, N., Vuorenmaa, E. and Mäki, M. 2018. *Kotitarveviljely ja hyötyeläimet Suomessa ja kotitarvetuotantoon vaikuttavat tekijät*. [Domestic food production and domestic animals in Finland and factors affecting domestic food production] Luonnonvara- ja biotalouden tutkimus 49/2018. Helsinki: Luonnonvarakeskus.

Koopmans, M. E., Keech, D., Sovová, L. and Reed, M. 2017. 'Urban agriculture and place-making: Narratives about place and space in Ghent, Brno and Bristol.' *Moravian Geographical Reports* 25(3), 154–165.

Kuivalainen, S. and Nelson, K. 2013. 'Eroding minimum income protection in the Nordic countries? Reassessing the Nordic model of social assistance.' In J. Kvist, J. Fritzell, B. Hvinden and O. Kangas (eds.). *Changing Social Equality. The Nordic Welfare Model in the 21st Century*. Bristol: Policy Press, 69–88.

Laamanen, M. 2017. *The Politics of Value Creation*. Helsinki: Hanken School of Economics.

Laclau, E. and Mouffe, C. 1985. *Hegemony and Socialist Strategy: Towards a Radical Democratic Politics*. London: Verso.

Laihiala, T. 2018. *Kokemuksia ja käsityksiä leipäjonosta: Huono-osaisuus, häpeä ja ansaitevuus*. [Disadvantagedness, shame and deservingness among the recipients of charity food aid in Finland]. Dissertations in Social Sciences and Business Studies. No 163. Kuopio: University of Eastern Finland.

Lal, R. 2004. 'Soil carbon sequestration impacts on global climate change and food security.' *Science* 304, 5677, 1623–1627.

Larsen, C. A. 2007. 'How welfare regimes generate and erode social capital. The impact of underclass phenomena.' *Comparative Politics* 40(1), 83–102.

Lasker, J. and Collom, E. 2011. 'Time banking and health: The role of a community currency organization in enhancing well-being.' *Health Promotion*

Practice 12(1), 102–115.

Light, A., and Miskelly, C. 2015. 'Sharing economy vs sharing cultures? Designing for social, economic and environmental good.' *Interaction Design and Architectures* 24, 49–62.

Lindsay, G. 2017. 'What if Uber kills off public transport rather than cars?' *The Guardian*. https://www.theguardian.com/sustainable-business/2017/jan/13/uber-lyft-cars-public-transport-cities-commuting (accessed 11 November 2018).

Linebaugh, P. 2008. *Magna Carta Manifesto. Liberties and Commons for All.* Berkeley: University of California Press.

LIPASTO 2018. 'Suomen tieliikenteen päästöjen kehitys.' [Development of the emissions from the Finnish road traffic.] *LIPASTO – calculation system for traffic exhaust emissions and energy use in Finland.* Updated 14 November 2018. http://lipasto.vtt.fi/liisa/aikasarja.htm (accessed 12 June 2019).

Lopes, M.L.A., Singer, H. and Justo, M.G. 2005. 'Economia Solidária e sistemas públicos: uma experiência de democracia em uma escola pública.' [Solidarity economy and public systems: an experience of democracy in a public school.] In Kruppa, S.M.P. (ed.) *Economia Solidária e educação de jovens e adultos.* [Solidarity economy and education of youth and adults.] Brasília: Inep/MEC, 69–81.

Lund, A. and Venäläinen, J. 2016. 'Monetary materialities of peer-produced knowledge: The case of Wikipedia and its tensions with paid labour.' *TripleC: Communication, Capitalism & Critique* 14(1), 78–98.

Macrotrends. 2018. 'Facebook operating expenses 2009–2018.' https://www.macrotrends.net/stocks/charts/FB/facebook/operating-expenses (accessed 8 December 2018).

Maderson, S. and Wynne-Jones, S. 2016. 'Beekeepers' knowledges and participation in pollinator conservation policy.' *Journal of Rural Studies* 45, 88–98.

Mandel, Ernest. 2010. 'Karl Marx.' In Eatwell, J., Milgate, M. and Newman, P. (eds.) *Marxian Economics*. Basingstoke: Palgrave Macmillan, 1–38.

Markussen, M.V., Kulak, M., Smith, L.G. and Nemecek, T. 2014. 'Evaluating the sustainability of a small-scale low-input organic vegetable supply system in the United Kingdom.' *Sustainability* 6, 1913–1945.

Martin, C. J. 2016. 'The sharing economy: A pathway to sustainability or a nightmarish form of neoliberal capitalism?' *Ecological Economics* 121, 149–159.

Mazzucato, M. 2018. *The Value of Everything. Making and Taking in the Global Economy.* UK: Allen Lane.

McCashin, A. 2016. 'How much change? Pierson and the welfare state revisited.' *Policy & Politics* 44(2), 313–329.

McIntyre, B.D., Herren, H.R., Wakhungu, J. and Watson, R.T. (eds.). 2009. *Agriculture at a Crossroads.* International Assessment of Agricultural Knowledge, Science and Technology for Development (IAASTD). Washington, DC: Island Press.

Merten, S. and Meretz, S. 2008. 'Germ form theory: Peer production in a historical perspective.' http://www.oekonux.org/texts/GermFormTheory.html (accessed 12 November 2018).

Mies, M. and Bennholdt-Thomsen, V. 1999. *The Subsistence Perspective. Beyond the Globalised Economy.* London: Zed Books.

Mikołajewska-Zając, K. 2016. 'Sharing as labour and as gift: Couchsurfing as an "affective enterprise".' *Ephemera* 16(4), 209–222.

Miller, E. 2004. 'Solidarity economics. Strategies for building new economies from the bottom-up and the inside-out.' *Grassroots Economic Organizing (GEO) Collective.* http://www.geo.coop/archives/SolidarityEconomicsEthanMiller.htm (accessed 13 June 2019).

Miller, E. 2013. 'Community economy: Ontology, ethics, and politics for radically democratic economic organizing.' *Rethinking Marxism* 25(4), 518–533.

Minas, R., Jakobsen, V., Kauppinen, T., Korpi, T., and Lorentzen, T. 2018. 'The governance of poverty: Welfare reform, activation policies, and social assistance benefits and caseloads in Nordic countries.' *Journal of European Social Policy* 28(5), 487–500.

Mitchell, T. 2007. 'Culture and economy.' In Bennett, T. and Frow, J. (eds.) *Handbook of Cultural Analysis.* London: Sage, 447–466.

Moberg, L. 2017. 'Marketisation of Nordic eldercare–Is the model still universal?.' *Journal of Social Policy* 46(3), 603–621.

Moore, L.J. and Kosut, M. 2013. *Buzz: Urban Beekeeping and the Power of the Bee.*

New York and London: New York University Press.

Moore, S.R. 2010. 'Energy efficiency in small-scale biointensive organic onion production in Pennsylvania, USA.' *Renewable Agriculture and Food Systems* 25(3), 181–188.

MoSAaH [The Ministry of Social Affairs and Health]. 2017.'STM: Suomalaisten osallisuuteen vaikutetaan ruoka-apua tehokkaammin varmistamalla yhteiskunnan rakenteiden toimivuus.' Press release. 21 December 2017. https://stm.fi/artikkeli/-/asset_publisher/stm-suomalaisten-osallisuuteen-vaikutetaan-ruoka-apua-tehokkaammin-varmistamalla-yhteiskunnan-rakenteiden-toimivuus (accessed 11 June 2019).

MoTC 2018a. *Hiiletön liikenne 2045 – polkuja päästöttömään tulevaisuuteen. Liikenteen ilmastopolitiikan työryhmän väliraportti.* [Carbon-free transport 2045 – Paths to an emission-free future. Interim report by the Transport Climate Policy Working Group.] Ministry of Transport and Communications. http://julkaisut.valtioneuvosto.fi/bitstream/handle/10024/161029/LVM_09_2018_Liikenteen_Ilmastopolitiikan_valiraportti.pdf?sequence=1&isAllowed=y

MoTC 2018b. *Toimenpideohjelma hiilettömään liikenteeseen 2045. Liikenteen ilmastopolitiikan työryhmä loppuraportti.* [Action programme for carbon-free transport 2045. Final report by the Transport Climate Policy Working Group.] Ministry of Transport and Communications. http://julkaisut.valtioneuvosto.fi/bitstream/handle/10024/161210/LVM_13_18_Toimenpideohjelma%20hiilettomaan%20liikenteeseen%202045%20Liikenteen%20ilmastopolitiikan%20tyoryhman%20loppuraportti.pdf?sequence=1&isAllowed=y

Nancy, J-L. 2000. *Being Singular Plural.* (Être singular pluriel) Translated to English by Robert D. Richardson and Anne E. O'Byrne. Stanford: Stanford University Press.

National Travel Survey 2012. 'Results.' [for the National Travel Survey 2010–2011.] *Finnish Transport Infrascture Agency.* https://vayla.fi/web/en/statistics/national-travel-survey/results#.XQKlmm_7SAx (accessed 13 June 2019).

Natural Resources Institute Finland. 2015. 'Mehiläistarhaus liittyi kannattavuuskirjanpitoon.' [Beekeeping joined the Farm Accountancy Data Network]. 27 April 2015. https://www.luke.fi/uutiset/mehilaistarhausliittyi-kannattavuuskirjanpitoon/ (accessed 18 December 2018).

Natural Resources Institute Finland. 2016a. 'Recreational use of nature.' https://www.luke.fi/en/natural-resources/recreational-use-of-nature/ (accessed 28 November 2018).

Natural Resources Institute Finland. 2016b. 'Recreational fishing.' https://www.luke.fi/en/natural-resources/fish-and-the-fishing-industry/recreational-fishing/ (accessed 28 November2018).

Neill, D. W., Fanning, A. L., Lamb, W. F. and Steinberger, J. K. 2018. 'A good life for all within planetary boundaries.' *Nature Sustainability* 1, 88–95.

Nelson, D.N. 2016. *Commons Democracy. Reading the Politics of Participation in the Early United States.* New York: Fordham University Press.

Niemi, P. and Pekkanen, P. 2016. 'Estimating the business potential for operators in a local food supply chain.' *British Food Journal* 118(11), 2815–2827.

Norse, D. 2003. 'Agriculture and the environment: changing pressures, solutions and trade-offs.' In Bruinsma, J. (ed.). *World Agriculture: Toward 2015/30 – An FAO Perspective.* FAO: Rome and London: Earthscan, 331–356.

North, P. 2007. *Money and Liberation: The Micropolitics of the Alternative Currency Movement.* Minneapolis: University of Minnesota Press.

Nousiainen, M., Pylkkänen, P., Saunders, F., Seppänen, L. and Vesanen, K.M. 2009. 'Are alternative food systems socially sustainable? A case study from Finland.' *Journal of Sustainable Agriculture* 33(5), 566–594.

Ohisalo, M., Laihiala, T. and Saari, J. 2015. 'Huono-osaisuuden ulottuvuudet ja kasautuminen leipäjonoissa.' [Dimensions and the accumulation of disadvantage in the breadline] *Yhteiskuntapolitiikka* 80(5), 435–446.

OSF [Official Statistics of Finland] 2018a. 'Participation in leisure activities.' http://www.stat.fi/til/vpa/index_en.html (accessed 18 December 2018).

OSF 2018b. 'Annual game bag.' http://www.stat.fi/til/riisaa/index_en.html (accessed 18.12.2018).

OSF 2018c. 'Producer prices of agricultural products.' http://www.stat.fi/til/matutu/index_en.html (accessed 18 December 2018).

OSF 2018d. 'Consumer price index.' http://www.stat.fi/til/khi/index_en.html (accessed 18 December 2018).

Parker, G., Van Alstyne, M., and Choudary, S. P. 2016. *Platform Revolution: How*

Networked Markets are Transforming the Economy and How to Make Them Work for You. New York: W. W. Norton & Company.

Parks, R., Baker, P., Kiser, L., Oakerson, R., Ostrom, E., Ostrom, V. and Percy, S. 1981. 'Consumers as co-producers of public services. Some economic and institutional considerations.' *Policy Studies Journal* 9(7), 1001–1011.

Peltonen, M. 1999. 'Työnjako sosiaalisena tilana – Sukupuolenmukaisesta työnjaosta maataloudessa.' [Division of labour as social space – on gendered division of labour in agriculture]. In Parikka, Raimo (ed.). *Suomalaisen työn historiaa. Korvesta konttoriin* [History of Work in Finland. From Backwoods to Office]. Suomalaisen kirjallisuuden seuran toimituksia 730. Helsinki: Finnish Literature Society, 33–50

Perkins, A. 2016. 'The death of hitchhiking is a modern tragedy.' *The Guardian.* https://www.theguardian.com/commentisfree/2016/sep/21/death-of-hitchhiking-modern-tragedy-frenchman-new-zealand (accessed 11 June 2019).

Plumwood, V. 1993. *Feminism and the Mastery of Nature.* London: Routledge.

Polanyi, K. (1944) 2001. *The Great Transformation: The Political and Economic Origins of Our Time.* Second Edition. Boston: Beacon Press Books.

Poppendieck, J. 1999. *Sweet Charity. Emergency Food and the End of Entitlement.* London: Penguin Books.

Prime Minister's Office Finland. 2018. *Eriarvoisuutta käsittelevän työryhmän loppuraportti* [Final report of a working group appointed to address inequality issues]. Valtioneuvoston kanslian julkaisusarja 1/2018. http://julkaisut.valtioneuvosto.fi/handle/10024/160706

Puig de la Bellacasa, M. 2017. *Matters of Care: Speculative Ethics in More Than Human Worlds.* Minneapolis: University of Minnesota Press.

Raffles, H. 2011. *Insectopedia.* New York: Vintage Books.

Ramos, J. M. 2016. 'The city as commons: A policy reader.' In: Ramos, José M. (ed.). *The City as Commons: A Policy Reader.* Melbourne: The Commons Transition Coalition, 1–12.

Ranta, E. 2014. *In the name of Vivir Bien. Indigeneity, state formation, and politics in Evo Morales' Bolivia.* PhD Thesis. Helsinki: University of Helsinki.

Bibliography

Rappe, E. 2005. *The Influence of a Green Environment and Horticultural Activities on the Subjective Well-Being of the Elderly Living in Long-Term Care.* PhD thesis. Helsinki: University of Helsinki.

Raworth, K. 2018. *Doughnut Economics: Seven Ways to Think Like a 21st-century Economist.* London: Random House.

Reimer, B. 2004. 'Social exclusion in a comparative context.' *Sociologica Ruralis* 44(1), 76–94.

Ricardo, D. 1817. *On the Principles of Political Economy and Taxation.* London: John Murray.

Robinson, G. 2004. *Geographies of Agriculture: Globalisation, Restructuring and Sustainability.* Abingdon: Routledge.

Robinson, J. 1962. *Economic Philosophy: An Essay on the Progress of Economic Thought.* London: C.A. Watts.

Robson, W. A. 1976. *Welfare State and Welfare Society. Illusion and Reality.* London: George Allen & Unwin.

Roelvink, G. 2015. 'Learning to be affected by earth others.' In K. Gibson, D. B. Rose and R. Fincher (eds.). *Manifesto for Living in the Anthropocene.* New York: punctum books, 57–62.

Rothstein, B. 2001. 'Social capital in the social democratic welfare state.' *Politics and Society* 29(2), 207–241.

Salonen, A.S. 2016. 'Christmas celebration of secondary consumers: Observations from food banks in Finland.' *Journal of Consumer Culture*, 16(3), 870–886.

Salonen, A. S. 2017. 'Religion, poverty, and abundance.' *Palgrave Communications* 4(27), 1–5.

Salonen, A. S., Ohisalo, M. and Laihiala, T. 2018. 'Undeserving, disadvantaged, disregarded: Three viewpoints of charity food aid recipients in Finland.' *International Journal of Environmental Research and Public Health. International Journal of Environmental Research and Public Health* 15(12), 2896.

Schandl, H., Hatfield-Dodds, S., Wiedmann, T., Geschke, A., Cai, Y., West, J., Newth, D., Baynes, T., Lenzen, M., and Owen, A. 2016. 'Decoupling global environmental pressure and economic growth: Scenarios for energy use, materials use and carbon emissions.' *Journal of Cleaner Production* 132, 45–56.

Schiller, H., Lekander, M., Rajaleid, K., Hellgren, C., Åkerstedt, T., Barck-

Holst, P., and Kecklund, G. 2018. 'Total workload and recovery in relation to worktime reduction: a randomised controlled intervention study with time-use data.' *Occupational and Environmental Medicine* 75(3), 218–226.

Schor, J. B. 2005. 'Sustainable consumption and worktime reduction.' *Journal of Industrial Ecology* 9(1–2), 37–50.

Schor, J. B. 2010. *Plenitude. The New Economics of True Wealth.* New York: The Penguin Press.

Schor, J. B. 2013. 'Why solving climate change requires working less.' In Coote, A. and Franklin, J. (eds.). *Time on Our Side: Why We All Need a Shorter Working Week.* London: New Economics Foundation, 3–20.

Schor, J. B. 2014. *Debating the Sharing Economy.* https://www.greattransition.org/publication/debating-the-sharing-economy (accessed 30 April 2019).

Sempik, J., Hine, R. and Wilcox, D. (eds.). 2010. *Green Care: A Conceptual Framework. A Report of the Working Group on the Health Benefits of Green Care.* COST 866, Green Care in Agriculture. Loughborough: Loughborough University.

Seyfang, G. 2004. 'Time banks: rewarding community self-help in the inner city?' *Community Development Journal* 39(1), 62–71.

Seyfang, G. and Smith, K. 2002. *The Time of Our Lives: Using Time Banking for Neighbourhood Renewal and Community Capacity Building.* London: New Economics Foundation.

SIES [Sistema de Informações em Economia Solidária] 2013. *Atlas Digital da Economia Solidária.* [Digital Atlas of Solidarity Economy.] http://atlas.sies.org.br/sobre.html (accessed 9 December 2018).

Silvasti, T. 2015. 'Normalising the abnormal in Finland.' *Social Policy & Society* 14(3), 471–482.

Silvasti, T. and Karjalainen, J. 2014. 'Hunger in a Nordic welfare state: Finland.' In T. Silvasti and G. Riches (eds.). *First World Hunger Revisited. Food Charity or the Right to Food.* London: Palgrave Maxmillan, 72–86.

Silvasti, T. and Riches, G. (eds.). 2014. *First World Hunger Revisited. Food Charity or the Right to Food.* London: Palgrave Macmillan.

Silvennoinen, K., Koivupuro, H-K., Katajajuuri, J-M., Jalkanen, L. and

Bibliography

Reinikainen, A. (2012) *Ruokahävikki suomalaisessa ruokakatjussa. Foodspill 2010–2012 -hankkeen loppuraportti. [Food waste in the Finnish food chain. Foodspill 2010–2012 -project final report]* MTT Report 41. Jokioinen: MTT.

Sipari, P. 2013. *Aarteenetsintää porkkanamaalla – Opettajien kokemuksia suomalaisten koulupuutarhojen toiminnasta ja ruokajärjestelmäopetuksesta* [Treasure hunting in the carrot bed – teachers' experiences in school gardening and food system education in Finland]. Master Thesis, University of Helsinki: Department of Geosciences and Geography. Helsinki: HELDA - Digital Repository of the University of Helsinki.

Smith, A. and Raven, R. 2012. 'What is protective space? Reconsidering niches in transitions to sustainability.' *Research Policy* 41(6), 1025–1103.

Smith, M. 2010. 'From big government to big society: Changing the state-society balance.' *Parliamentary Affairs* 63(4), 818–833.

Smith, T. S. J. 2018. *Sustainability, Wellbeing and the Posthuman Turn*. London: Palgrave Macmillan.

Snyder, D. 2015. *Commercial Capital and the Political Economy of Agricultural Overproduction*. PhD Thesis. Syracuse University: Department of Political Science. Syracuse: SURFACE.

Standing, G. 2009. *Work after Globalization: Building Occupational Citizenship*. Cheltenham: Edward Elgar Publishing.

Statista. 2018. 'Forecast of Facebook user numbers in Finland from 2015 to 2021(in million users).' https://www.statista.com/statistics/568778/forecast-of-facebook-user-numbers-in-finland/ (accessed 8 December 2018).

Statistics Finland. 2018a. 'Kasvihuonekaasupäästöt Suomessa muuttujina Vuosi, Päästöluokka, Kasvihuonekaasu ja Tiedot.' [Greenhouse gas emissions in Finland as variables Year, Emission class, Greenhouse gas and Data]. https://pxnet2.stat.fi/PXWeb/pxweb/fi/StatFin/StatFin__ymp__khki/statfin_khki_pxt_111k.px (accessed 12 November 2018).

Statistics Finland. 2018b. 'Motor vehicle stock [e-publication].' Helsinki: Statistics Finland. https://www.stat.fi/til/mkan/2018/mkan_2018_2019-03-22_tie_001_en.html (accessed 6 June 2019).

Stavrides, S. 2016. *Common Space. The city as Commons*. London: Zed Books.

Stephens, L., Ryan-Collins, J. and Boyle, D. 2008. *Co-Production: A Manifesto for Growing the Core Economy*. London: New Economics Foundation.

Stewart, Bob. 2011. 'The golden age of hitchhiking.' *Alabama Humanities Foundation.* http://www.alabamahumanities.org/the-golden-age-of-hitchhiking/ (accessed 6 June 2019).

Sundararajan, A. 2016. *The Sharing Economy: The End of Employment and the Rise of Crowd-Bbased Capitalism.* Cambridge: The MIT Press.

Svallfors, S. 2012. 'Welfare states and welfare attitudes.' In Svallfors, S. (ed.) *Contested Welfare States: Welfare Attitudes in Europe and Beyond.* Stanford: Stanford University Press, 1–24.

Tanska, T. 2018. *Leipäjonojen uudistaminen – asiakasnäkökulma : Helsingin leipäjonojen asiakaskyselyn tulokset [Renewingg breadlines – a customer point of view: Results of a customer survey of Helsinki Breadlines].* Helsinki: FinFami Uusimaa ry. https://www.finfamiuusimaa.fi/wp-content/uploads/sites/12/Leip%C3%A4jonojen_uudistaminen_2018_asiakasn%C3%A4k%C3%B6kulma.pdf

Theocarakis, N.J. 2010. 'Metamorphoses: The Concept of labour in the history of political economy.' *The Economic and Labour Relations Review* 20(2), 7–37.

Timonen, P. 2005. 'Iloa ja nautintoja kotitöistä' [Joy and pleasure from domestic work]. *Hyvinvointikatsaus* 2/2005, 4–7.

Trafi [Finnish Transport Safety Agency]. 2017. 'Open data at Trafi.' https://www.trafi.fi/en/information_services/open_data (accessed 12 November.2018).

Trauger, A. and Passidomo, C. 2012. 'Towards a post-capitalist-politics of food: Cultivating subjects of community economies.' *ACME: An International E-Journal for Critical Geographies* 11(2), 282–303.

Trommer, S., Kolarova, V., Fraedrich, E., Kröger, L., Kickhöfer, B., Kuhnimhof, T., Lenz, B., Phleps, P. 2016. 'Autonomous driving – The impact of vehicle automation on mobility behaviour.' München: Institute for Mobility Research. http://www.ifmo.de/publications.html?t=45

Tsing, A.L. 2015. *The Mushroom at the End of the World: On the Possibility of Life in Capitalist Ruins.* Princeton: Princeton University Press.

Utting, P. (ed.). 2015. *Social and Solidarity Economy Beyond the Fringe.* London: Zed Books.

Vermeulen, S.J., Campbell, B.M., Ingram, J.S I. 2012. 'Climate change and food systems.' *Annual Review of Environment and Resources* 37, 195–222.

Bibliography

Victor, P. A. 2012. 'Growth, degrowth and climate change: A scenario analysis.' *Ecological Economics* 84, 206–212.

Wanderley, F. (Coord.), Sostres, F. and Farah, I. 2015. *La economía solidaria en la economía plural. Discursos, prácticas y resultados en Bolivia.* [The solidarity economy in the plural economy. Discourses, practices and results in Bolivia.] La Paz, Bolivia: CIDES-UMSA.

White, R. J. and Williams C. 2016. 'Beyond capitalocentricism: are non-capitalist work practices "alternatives"?' *Area* 48(3), 325–331.

Whiteley, P. F. 2000. 'Economic growth and social capital.' *Political Studies* 48, 443–466.

World Bank. 1998. *The Initiative on Defining, Monitoring and Measuring Social Capital. Overview and Program Description.* Social Capital Initiative, Working Paper 1.

World Resources Institute. 2018. *Creating a Sustainable Food Future. A Menu of Solutions to Feed Nearly 10 Billion People by 2050.* Synthesis Report, December 2018. Washington, DC: World Resources Institute.

Wright, E. O. 2011. 'Real utopias.' *Contexts* 10(2), 36–42.

Wright, E.O. 2013. 'Transforming capitalism through real utopias.' *American Sociological Review* 78(1), 1–25.

Wright, S. 2010. 'Cultivating beyond-capitalist economies.' *Economic Geography* 86(3), 297–318.

YCharts. 2018. 'Facebook Inc market cap: 34.92B for Dec. 7, 2018.' https://ycharts.com/companies/FB/market_cap (accessed 8 December 2018).

Ylitalo, M. 2008. 'Luontoisetuina gourmet-tason makuelämyksiä – Suuria alueittaisia eroja luonnon antimien keräämisessä' [Gourmet level taste experiences as a fringe benefit – Large regional differences in collecting nature products]. *Kuntapuntari* 1/2008. https://www.stat.fi/artikkelit/2008/art_2008-05-08_002.html (accessed 30 November 2018).

www.ingramcontent.com/pod-product-compliance
Lightning Source LLC
Chambersburg PA
CBHW060530100426
42743CB00009B/1480